Squirrel Trouble

VOLUME TWO
Filbert the Flying Whale

Written by **Allen Swim**
Illustrated by **Andrew Scully**

Copyright © 2016
Allen Swim
All rights reserved. No part of this book may be reproduced in any form — except for the inclusion of brief quotations in review — without permission in writing from the author.
ISBN: 978-1540811899

For My Jeffrey
Without whom, I am only a fraction of myself.

BOOKS BY ALLEN SWIM

FILBERT, FLOATING ON AIR
Volume One
Filbert the Flying Whale

•

SQUIRREL TROUBLE
Volume Two
Filbert the Flying Whale

•

THE RISE OF BOO BOO FORCE
Volume Three
Filbert the Flying Whale
Coming Soon

•

FRED THE TURTLE
(A picture book in collaboration with Andrew Scully)

CHAPTER 1

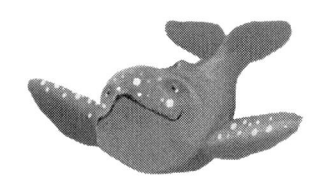

Hard Sweet Rain

"Okay, Lulu, let 'er rip!" shouted Filbert to the small red-haired girl riding on his back. They soared high over Dirty Dog Park, the wind roaring in their ears. Standing with her feet apart and knees slightly bent, Lulu rode Filbert more like a skateboard than a 10-foot-long 1,000-pound gray whale.

Lulu tore open a bag of Fruity Booty and dumped it out, sending the colorful little blocks of fruit-flavored hard candy plummeting toward the unsuspecting squirrels below. Tearing and dumping bag after bag, she worked, her hands a blur, laughing hysterically the entire time. "Ha ha! Once they see who gave them all this great candy, they'll forget about the soccer field," shouted Lulu.

"I hope so," said Filbert. When he'd first encountered the squirrels, Filbert had unintentionally destroyed their soccer field. He and Lulu came up with the idea of giving them candy as a way to apologize.

"That's the last of the candy, Fil!" Lulu had to yell over the rush of the wind.

Hovering overhead, Filbert and Lulu could hear the sounds below. It was a radiant summer day and the park was abuzz with laughter. A giddy sense of expectation bubbled up inside of Filbert. "They're going to be so happy."

The tasty blocks of candy sparkled in the sunshine. Green, red, yellow, blue, purple, and orange circles began to appear all around the squirrels. Little paws reached up to touch the strange shafts of light. Oohs and aahs could be heard coming from their smiling furry faces.

Picking up speed, the Fruity Booty whistled and spun like tiny bombs streaking toward the earth. The first piece of candy struck right in the middle of a buffet table. *KABLAMMO!* It exploded into shards of sugary sweetness. Shrieking squirrels scrambled for cover. Filbert's joy changed to horror as he watched helplessly.

"Take cover!"

"Help us!"

"Someone save me a bagel!"

The candy crashed down with a vengeance, exploding into sparkling clouds of sugary sweet vapor. *CRACK! SPLAT! POW! BOOM! SMASH! SQUAT!* Squirrels were knocked to the ground or thrown into the air, the candy turning their fur all variety of colors.

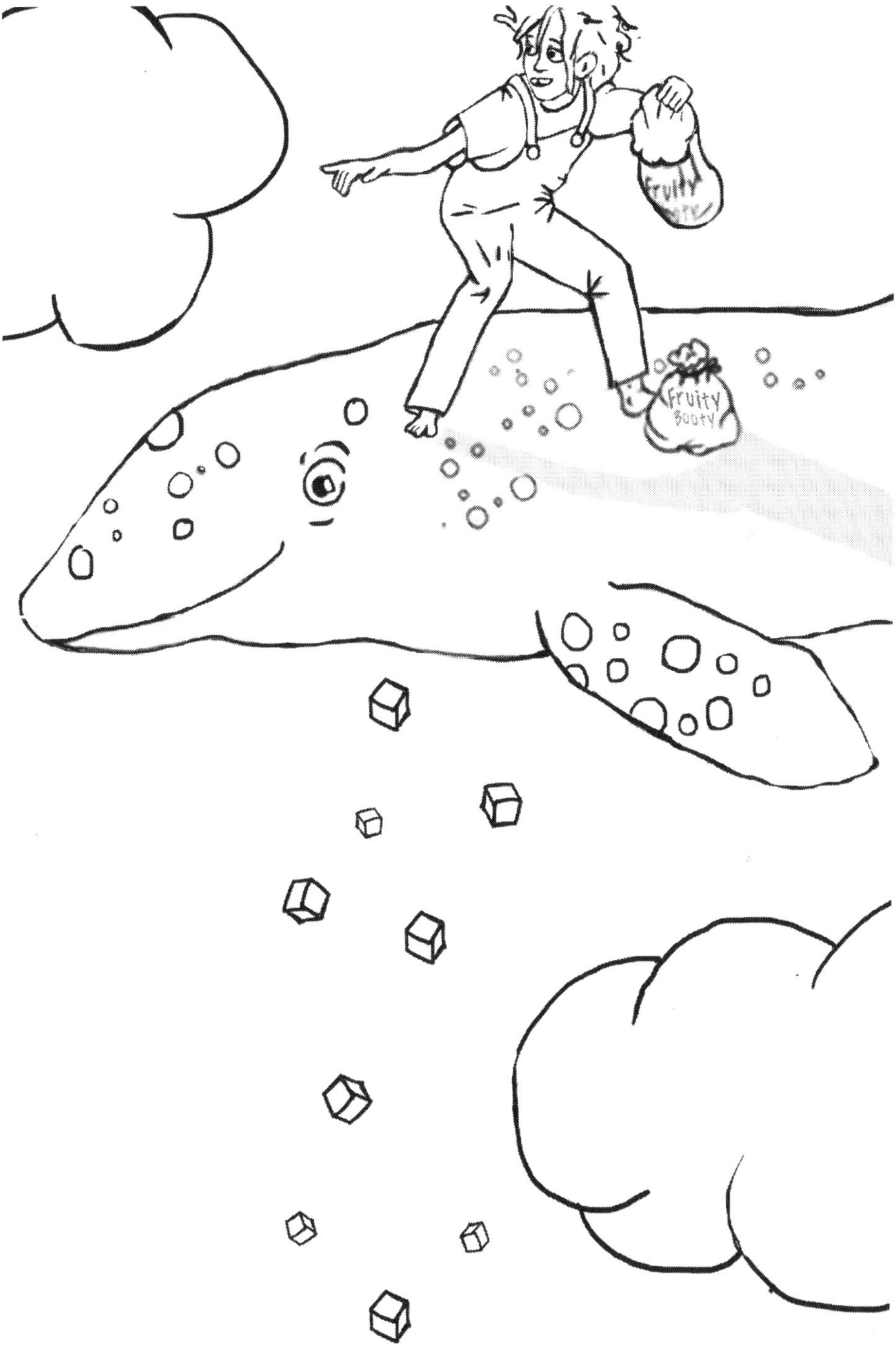
Fruity Booty
Fruity Booty

Squirrel Trouble

For the squirrels in the lake, the results were no less devastating. Candy impacts caused geysers to rise from the water, spewing swimmers into the air.

"Oh no. What've we done?" asked Lulu.

"We've got to go down there and help!" exclaimed Filbert.

"I don't know, Fil. Someone might see us."

"We have to try," insisted Filbert.

The sight of a flying whale frightened most humans. Whenever they saw Filbert, people called the police. Lulu's father, Cornelius, was working on an idea that would allow Filbert to fly around The City without anyone bothering him. Cornelius warned them not to risk getting captured because it could interfere with his plan.

Dazed, most of the squirrels had no idea what hit them. Filbert and Lulu could hear their confused chattering as they approached.

One squirrel looked up and shouted, "Look! It's that evil flying whale. He did this to us!"

"Destroyer!" shouted the squirrels in unison, pointing at Filbert and Lulu.

"No, we were just trying to be nice," said Filbert.

"You smashed our swim meet!"

"I'm so sorry," cried Filbert.

"We've heard that before. Just leave us alone, Destroyer."

"Boo! Go home! Destroyer!"

"We should go, Fil. We're way too close to the ground. People are going to see us," cautioned Lulu.

Filbert and Lulu flew away.

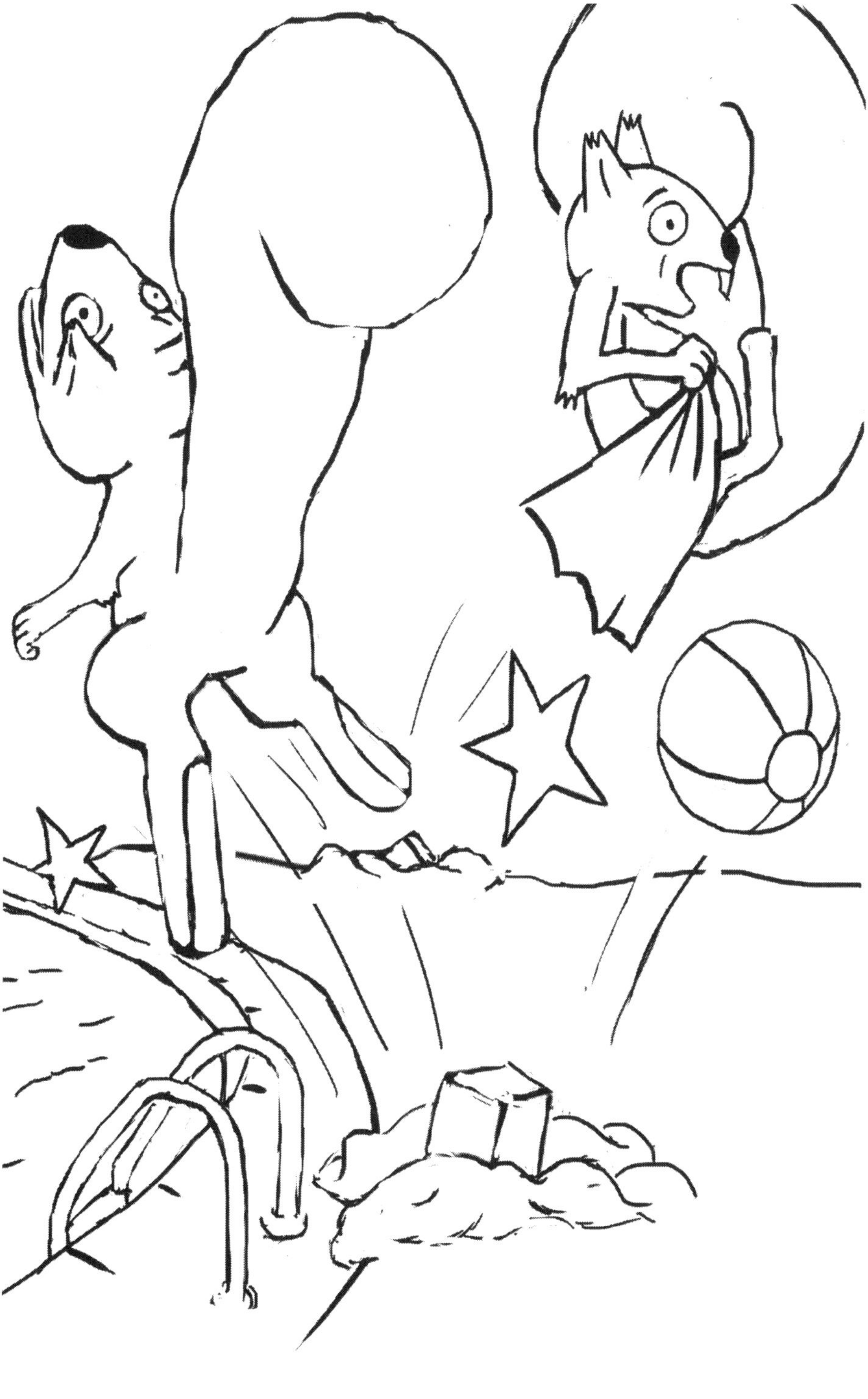

Squirrel Trouble

"I wish there was something I could do," said Filbert. "Maybe we could drop some water on the really sticky ones?"

"No, Fil," said Lulu, patting Filbert on the head. "There's nothing we can do, except learn from our mistake."

"Never again will we bombard unsuspecting rodents with hard candy," agreed Filbert solemnly.

On their way back to Lulu's house, Filbert dashed from cloud to cloud trying to stay out of sight.

"This is taking sooo long," complained Lulu. "Why didn't you wish to be invisible too?"

"I wasn't thinking about hiding from humans. I wanted to meet people and make new friends. Besides, that genie was in a foul mood. I'm lucky I even got one wish."

"You're the one who freed him from that stinky old chest, right?" Before Filbert could answer, Lulu continued. "He would still be trapped down there if you didn't come along."

They came upon a small tree-shrouded neighborhood. At the end of the street was a green-and-blue house with red polka dots all over it. Filbert flew around to the back. A two-story chicken coop sat in the middle of the yard. Gunther the rooster was lying in a wooden lounge chair, a towel draped over his face. He wore gym shorts and a white tank top.

"Welcome home, young lady," said Gunther. "Your father has been looking for you."

"We were buying socks," said Lulu.

"You better go see Cornelius right away. He's super upset."

A feeling of dread came over Filbert. Lulu went into the house looking for Cornelius. A few minutes later she returned.

Hard Sweet Rain

"I can't find him anywhere. Let's check his workshop." She led Filbert to a giant orange building out behind the chicken coop.

Cornelius's workshop looked like an enormous garage with large double doors. Lulu pulled a remote control from her pocket and the doors swung outward. Inside, there were stacks of boxes and equipment everywhere. Off to one side were a forklift and a snowplow.

"Daddy? Hello?" called Lulu. "He might be on the lower level."

Lulu headed for a ramp that led down to a spacious hallway. Filbert followed closely behind. Halfway down, the clinking and clunking of tools could be heard.

At the bottom of the ramp, the hallway was dimly lit by a single light bulb. It led to an iron door. As the pair approached, the banging of metal on metal grew louder. *CLINK, BANG, TINK!* Just as Lulu was turning the doorknob, she heard a meaty *thunk!*

"OWWW! RATSTAB CRACKLESNAPPER!" screeched Cornelius.

They slid open the heavy door and saw Cornelius hopping up and down, shaking his left hand wildly. He wore a white lab coat and a scarf of chicken feathers. The coat flapped like a turkey wing, and from his scarf a cloud of feathers sprinkled down around him like confetti. His white hair was littered with the dark plumage.

"Hit your hand again, Daddy?" asked Lulu.

"Never mind that. Where have you been?" asked Cornelius accusingly.

"I was in the hen house. I have no idea where Lulu was," blurted Filbert.

"Come now, Filbert. I searched everywhere for you two."

"Are we in trouble?"

"We just wanted to go out for a little bit," interjected Lulu, before Cornelius could answer. "We were really careful and

Hard Sweet Rain

nothing happened," said Lulu, giving Filbert a wink, a nod, and a sneaky nudge with her elbow.

"Yes, yes," lied Filbert. "Absolutely nothing." At first, Filbert was confused by Lulu's wink and nod. It took that sneaky nudge to help him realize that Lulu wanted him to back her up. Considering the fiasco that operation "Sweet Squirrel" turned out to be, it was quite a stretch to say nothing had happened while they were out.

"If this continues to happen, there will be no more play dates for you two," said Cornelius. Filbert and Lulu both gasped dramatically. "I know it seems harsh, but you're 8 years old. Old enough to start taking responsibility for your actions. Don't you think?"

"Yes sir," said Filbert and Lulu in unison.

"Good. Now, let's move on to something more positive," said Cornelius. "If all goes according to my plan, Filbert, you'll be free to roam around The City by this time next week."

"What's this plan?" asked Filbert. Cornelius explained. In order to make it legal for Filbert to fly around The City, Filbert had to be registered. So Cornelius applied for a license to take his pet flying whale for walks. The City Council was willing to grant his request, as long as Filbert passed a safety inspection. They would be sending an agent out next week. If Filbert passed the inspection, he would be allowed to fly around The City with either Lulu or Cornelius.

"So, I would be your pet?" asked Filbert.

"Only in the eyes of The City. What it really means is that we would be responsible for your actions. Like making sure

Squirrel Trouble

you don't bite anyone's face off and stuff like that."

"Good job, Daddy," said Lulu.

"Just make sure that you're here by noon on Tuesday, so you can meet the inspector," said Cornelius.

"I'll be here."

"Alright, children, I need to get back to work," said Cornelius.

They said their good-byes and Filbert set off for home.

CHAPTER 2

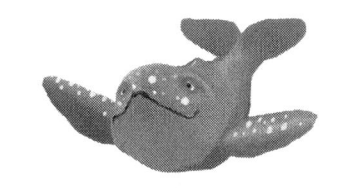

Giant Clams

Filbert floated groggily into the kitchen, where his mother was sautéing some fresh chum. "Good morning, sleepyhead," said Mother. "Or should I say afternoon?" Being an adult gray whale, Edweena was huge. She was dark gray with white splotches all over her body. Weighing over 70,000 pounds and stretching close to 50 feet long, she dwarfed Filbert. He looked like a tiny gray pickle next to her.

"Is it that late already?" asked Filbert. It was a lot of work, sneaking around on land. He'd had to flee three different packs of humans on his way home last night. Filbert slurped greedily at the food Edweena set in front of him.

"I'm worried about you, all this sneaking around and running from humans. I think it might be too dangerous for you to visit Lulu anymore."

Squirrel Trouble

"They'll never catch me," said Filbert, his mouth stuffed with food. "It doesn't matter anyway. Cornelius has figured out a way to make them leave me alone." He went on to explain the idea about getting a license.

Edweena was wary, but with a little begging from her son, she said, "Okay, honey. But we'll have to discuss this with your father."

"Where's Roger?" asked Filbert. Ever since Filbert revealed that he could fly, he and his brother Roger had been spending less and less time together.

"Your brother is outside with the clams. It was your turn to take them for a drag this morning."

"Roger doesn't mind. He loves Smeepy and Smarple."

"That's not the point. It's about taking responsibility. When we got those clams, you both promised to take care of them."

"Yes, Mama. I'll go out and help Roger right now."

Outside, Filbert found his twin brother returning from exercising their new pets. Roger had green and purple alternating stripes running the length of his body. His face and head were covered in red polka dots. Other than the coloring differences, the two young whales were identical, both 10 feet long and exactly 1,013 pounds. Roger dragged two giant clams into the yard, holding a leash in each fin. The clams were bluish-green on the outside, but inside, they were just a gross gray and white mash-up of slimy guts and stuff.

When the clams saw Filbert they started barking and hopping up and down. Jumping all over him, they gave Filbert friendly little nips on his neck and spine. Laughing,

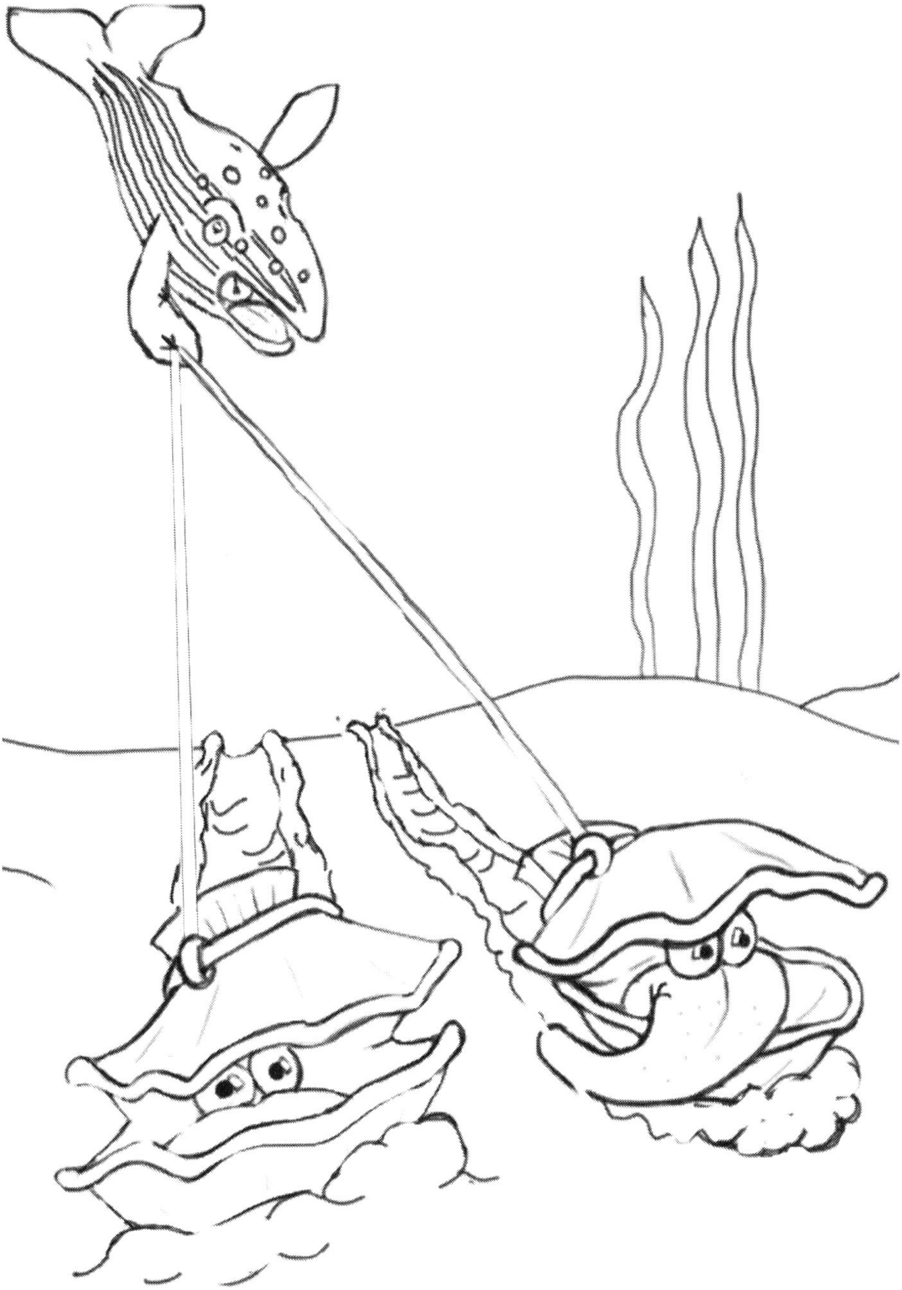

Squirrel Trouble

Filbert grabbed one clam in a big hug and headbutted the other one into the ground. Both clams started to purr.

"Filbert!" exclaimed Roger. "Be careful, Smeepy hates when you do that."

"I headbutt Smeepy every time I see him. That's our thing," protested Filbert.

"Not the headbutt. It's the hugging. You know that old saying: Hold a clam, fry your ham."

"I don't know that saying."

"Okay, but Smeepy bit me pretty good last time I picked him up."

"That's just because they don't like you," said Filbert with a grin. It was hard to keep from making fun of Roger; he was such an easy target.

Irritated, Roger said, "They *do* like me! Watch. Come here boys, come on." The two clams paid him no attention.

"Go on," said Filbert, motioning toward Roger. Both clams bounded back to Roger instantly. "See?"

"Whatever. I'm the one who takes care of them all the time. How could they like you more? You're never around anyway," said Roger.

Filbert felt bad. He *had* been spending a lot of time with Lulu. "I'm here now. Let's get these filthy pigs cleaned up."

"Pigs?" said Roger.

"They're like flounders, but with legs and hard feet called hooves," explained Filbert.

The boys washed their clams thoroughly. Roger scrubbed Smeepy and Smarple with fried rice and a two-handed long

Giant Clams

sword. Smacking them with his tail as hard as he could, Filbert knocked the rice right out of them. In the end, the clams were happy, shiny, and clean. Roger tried to coax them into their clam house, but they wouldn't budge until Filbert whistled and pointed, and the two clams dutifully obeyed.

"Filbert, Roger, it's time for Whale Song," called Richard, the boys' father. Richard was mostly dark gray with areas of lighter gray dispersed over his body. He had the same white splotches as Edweena and Filbert. He also had a single orange dot over his left eye. Being half gray whale and half pilot whale, he was smaller than his wife. Richard was only 35 feet long and weighed about 50,000 pounds.

"Can we take the clams?" shouted Roger.

"As long as you keep them tied up," answered Richard.

"Yay!" shouted the boys. They each took a clam by the leash and the family rushed off to Whale Song.

Whale Song was an ancient ritual that all the whales from Filbert's town, Deep End, participated in on a daily basis. It was said, when the first whales came to Earth over 40 million years ago, the ritual was created to show whale unity.

Arriving at the center of town, the boys tied up Smeepy and Smarple and hurried to take their places with the other whale children. Hundreds of whales were gathered together. There were gray whales and blue whales, pilot and killer whales, and many more. Everyone had a place. They started by separating into six different groups. Males and females were separated, then adults and children. The adult groups were further split into parents and non-parents.

Squirrel Trouble

High-pitched screeches and swaying bodies marked the beginning. Each group sang and danced separately. One by one they joined. Soon the entire community was wailing and dancing together. Sounds and movements became one, building and building to a crescendo until the entire assembly was a single entity. It ended abruptly on a final earsplitting note. There was no leader; no one gave a signal, everyone just knew when it was over, instinctively. Once Whale Song ended, the whales went about their daily business.

Many of the gray whale children liked to hang out with Filbert and Roger. This had not always been the case. Being part pilot whale, Filbert and Roger were much smaller than the other children. Because of this, for a long time the two brothers were outcasts from the gray whales and spent most of their time alone or playing only with each other. That all changed after Filbert started flying. He became a whale celebrity, and the brothers were welcomed by the other gray whale children and soon had many friends.

The children loved to listen to Filbert tell stories about going on land and interacting with humans.

"Tell us about your friend Lulu," said Megan. She was younger than Filbert and Roger, but already 17 feet long and weighed over 4,000 pounds.

"No, tell us about how you beat that hawk and saved the chicken," shouted Charlie. He was the biggest and strongest of all the gray whale kids, weighing 23,000 pounds and stretching 25 feet in length. He had lots of scars from roughhousing with the sharks that lived nearby. When he spoke, everyone listened.

Filbert started to tell his story when Roger came floating up with Smeepy and Smarple. The clams were an instant hit; everyone wanted to pet them. They were purring and yipping with joy. Smarple fastened himself to Charlie's back and was buzzing like a tree frog as he rode the whale. The kids exploded with questions.

"Are they yours?"

"When did you get them?"

"They're so soft and shiny!"

"Does 3 x 12 = 36?"

Filbert was a little upset that Roger had taken all the kids away from his story, but after a moment, he was actually happy that his brother was getting some attention, too. Filbert smiled.

"No, not yet," said Roger, to a kid who asked if the clams knew any tricks. "I've been trying to teach them to play dead and roll over, but they just don't seem to understand."

Filbert couldn't help himself. "They understand, they just don't like Roger very much," he said. All the kids laughed.

"Yes, they do," said Roger, through gritted teeth. Trying to control his anger, Roger smiled and leaned over to give Smeepy a kiss. Smeepy jumped up, bit Roger, and held tightly to his face. "AAAAKKK!" howled Roger and tried to shake the clam free. Smarple growled and jumped on his back, nipping at him. Roger danced around, hooting and hollering with the clams hanging on him, until Filbert came to his rescue.

Squirrel Trouble

The dots on Roger's face were bright red with embarrassment. Megan suggested using treats to reward the clams during training.

"I have some Fishy Fingers," said Matthew. He offered the deep-fried candied treats to Roger.

Using the Fishy Fingers, Roger was able to get Smeepy and Smarple to do many tricks. They rolled over, barked on command, played dead, and even made a small automobile out of some rocks, driftwood, and a potato. Every time they did a trick, Roger would toss them a bit of Fishy Finger. After about 20 or so tricks, Smeepy made an indecent sound. *SSSPPPLLLAAARRT!* Then Smarple did too. *SSSPPLLEERRT!* Soon the two clams were ripping burps and farts all over the place. *PLART! POOT! SQUEAKER!*

Disgusted, the other kids quickly swam off.

"I guess we shouldn't have fed them so much," said Roger.

Filbert and Roger dragged the gaseous beasts back home, holding their breath the entire way. After putting their clams away, Filbert and Roger rejoined their friends for a game of dirt in your eye. The game mostly consisted of throwing mud in the faces of the other players.

When it came time to pick teams, Filbert was always picked first because he could fly. Roger was picked last because he was so small. The silly thing was that being able to fly didn't help Filbert in games that were played underwater. Whispering in his team captain's ear, Filbert made sure Roger was picked next, even before Charlie, who

Giant Clams

was the best player. Roger's smile was worth every bit of mud slapped in Filbert's face. By the time the fourth game started, the two brothers had learned to work together and were quite good. The young whales played until dark.

At home, the boys were greeted by their father. He had a few questions about Cornelius's idea. Mainly, he wanted to know what the inspection consisted of. Filbert was so excited about the idea that he had forgotten to ask. Richard told Filbert to be sure to find out. Filbert wasn't worried, but he agreed to ask Cornelius about it the next day.

Edweena was still very concerned about Filbert being chased by the humans. She and Richard exchanged some heated words on the subject. Richard finished by saying, "Filbert isn't a baby anymore. We have to let him grow up." In the end, she grudgingly agreed to allow Filbert to attend the inspection.

After dinner, the brothers cleaned up the dishes, brushed their teeth, and wrestled around until Father had to tell them to "KNOCK IT OFF!" They finally got into bed and Mom came in to say goodnight and tucked them in.

"You sure are brave, Fil," said Roger.

"What are you talking about?" he asked.

"I would be scared to take that test."

"Test? Do you mean for the license?"

"Yeah."

"It's not a test, you stinky monkey. It's an inspection. Why should I be scared of that?"

Squirrel Trouble

"They'll probably stick you with a bunch of needles and hit you with a hammer or something like that."

"That's just ridiculous, Roger."

"I don't know, Snarlfoot told me about a guy who had to pass an inspection for the humans and they made him eat terrible things until he threw up."

"He never told you anything like that. Plus, you said that Snarlfoot was just a crazy seagull."

"Sometimes he's right. You know that saying Dad has. Even a fat fish likes to lie in the river."

Filbert was irritated by Roger's foolishness. "That's not a saying," he said, rolling his eyes.

"Humans are wild animals; you never know what they'll do. They might say mean things to you or turn you into crayons or something."

Even though it seemed silly, Filbert realized that his brother was just worried about him. His tone softened. "Don't worry, Roger. I promise I'll be careful. Now go to sleep."

Filbert lay awake in his bed. He couldn't stop thinking about the inspection. After a little while, Roger started to snore, loudly. Filbert got up and went to the bathroom for some tissue. Ever so quietly, he stuffed the tissue into Roger's blowhole. He rushed back to his bed holding in a laugh. Roger woke up coughing and found the tissue.

"Hey! That's not funny!" shouted Roger.

Filbert pretended to be asleep at first, but he couldn't hold in his giggles any longer. He burst out laughing and Roger threw the tissue at him.

Giant Clams

"You ugly crab! I'm telling Mom," threatened Roger.

Filbert just laughed. When he finally fell asleep, he dreamed he was in a cage being poked and prodded by humans all night long.

CHAPTER 3

Donkey and the Tiniest Pig

The next day Filbert woke to find Smeepy and Smarple in his bed. They were barking and jumping up and down on him. The two clams knocked him to the floor and proceeded to sit on his head and lick his face.

"Yuck!" shouted Filbert. "Who let these dirty clams in?" Pushing them off, Filbert caught a quick glimpse of Roger's tail as he rushed out of the room, laughing hysterically. "Arrgh! My bed is full of sand!" Filbert was in too much of a hurry to even bother trying to get revenge. Besides, it *was* pretty funny.

On the way to Lulu's house, Filbert flew higher than usual, remembering Cornelius's warning not to be seen by humans. Unfortunately, at that height everything on the ground was

Donkey and the Tiniest Pig

just a blur. Filbert had to come back down closer to Earth so that he could see where he was going. Once he got to Dirty Dog Park, he gave it a wide berth in order to avoid the squirrels. Lulu's house was tucked into a small valley on the other side of the park.

Filbert found Lulu in the backyard. She was standing face to face with Gunther the rooster. They were both dressed all in white. Each wore a silvery metal mesh face mask that had padded material covering their necks. In their hands were long, thin swords. The end of each sword had a plastic cap on the tip. A crowd of hens watched the action.

Lulu and Gunther saluted each other and had at it. The rooster swung his sword at Lulu, who easily knocked it aside with a metallic *clink*. Back and forth they struggled, swiping and stabbing at each other. Gunther grunted with each thrust and parry. The sound of the swords echoed as they came together, again and again. *Clink clack! Clink clack!*

"Aha! Ho! He!" shouted the fiery-haired little girl.

The battle was even until Lulu swung her sword too wide and lost her balance. Gunther quickly took advantage, jabbing her in the stomach before she could recover. The chickens roared with delight, cheering for the rooster.

"Fine duel, sir," said Lulu formally. "Thank you for the lesson."

"My pleasure, Lulu," returned Gunther.

The rooster turned to say hello to Filbert and Lulu gave him a stinging whap on the butt with her sword.

"Yikes!" Gunther yelped.

Squirrel Trouble

Everyone laughed. Lulu was not known for her grace in defeat.

"Hey, Fil. I wasn't expecting you until Tuesday," said Lulu, turning to greet the whale.

"I came to talk with your father."

"He's working, but he takes a break around noon. Do you want to play until then?"

"Excellent idea!"

"Let me put my fencing stuff away."

"Fencing stuff?" said Filbert, puzzled.

"My sword-fighting gear. It's called fencing."

Filbert floated up to the window of Lulu's room. Inside, the walls were each painted a different color: red, blue, orange, and green. On one side of the room, the carpet was pink; on the other side, it was blue. The pink side was frilly and lacy. The blue side was sporty and rough and looked a little dirty. Lulu's bed was on the pink side and had posters of horses and rainbows over it. On the blue side sat an old battered footlocker and the walls had pictures of rock bands and sports teams. It was hard to explain, but Filbert got two distinctly different feelings from each side. The pink side made him want to hug an antelope and take care of orphaned kittens. The blue side gave him a sense of excitement and fear.

The door opened and Lulu walked into the room wearing a pink dress. She grabbed the edge of the blue wall and pulled it back. To Filbert's surprise, the blue wall wasn't a wall at all; it was a big blue tarp that concealed a closet behind it. Lulu threw her fencing equipment into the closet, put the tarp back in place and started rummaging around in the old footlocker. Pulling out a large water cannon, she ran over to the window.

"What did you want to talk to Daddy about?" asked Lulu, cranking open the window.

"Well, I was wondering what the safety inspection would be like," said Filbert.

"They'll probably scrape off the first couple of layers of your skin and dip you in acid," said Lulu.

"What?!" exclaimed Filbert.

Lulu laughed so hard that she fell on the floor. "No, not really. It won't be a big deal."

"Excuse me, Lulu," called Gunther from the yard below. "I believe you owe me an apology for that swat on my rear end."

"You're right. I'm sorry, Gunther."

"Apology accepted. Might I offer some advice on fencing?"

"I guess so."

"You should always remember not to overreach when attacking an opponent. Especially when facing one with superior skills," said the rooster.

Filbert could see Lulu's expression change at Gunther's last remark. Her eye started to twitch and she looked as if she could choke a small mouse. She raised the water cannon, taking careful aim at Gunther.

Gunther's eyes grew wide; he just stood there, staring up at Lulu.

Squirrel Trouble

"Don't do it, Lulu," said Filbert.

She lowered the water cannon and let out a sigh. The rooster quickly disappeared.

"I thought you were going to blast him," said Filbert.

"I was, but Daddy says that I have to try to control my temper. He's just so full of himself! 'Superior skills,' yeah right! I'm sorry that I didn't give him *two* whacks. One for each cheek!"

"You did the right thing, Lulu. I don't think he meant to be insulting. You know how chickens are," said Filbert.

"Yeah, I guess so."

"We should just leave this here," said Filbert, taking the water cannon from Lulu and setting it down on the floor.

Lulu came back outside and suggested that they play World Traveler. In the game, Lulu was on vacation and Filbert played the different people she met. He started out playing a young Mexican girl selling donuts by a giant rabbit hole. Eventually he finished up acting the part of a 76-year-old llama from Hoovesville, Indiana.

At the end of the game Lulu said, "It's almost lunch time; we should go find Daddy so you can talk to him." The pair crossed the yard and headed for Cornelius's workshop. As they reached the door, a cry of alarm came from the chicken coop.

"They're back! Take cover!"

Filbert spun around just in time to see a tall gray donkey come around the side of the house. Sitting on the back of the donkey was a small blond boy wearing a red cape and holding a large butterfly net. The donkey charged into the crowd of panicked chickens. Whooping and hollering like a savage hedgehog, the boy swung his net, further scattering the frenzied chickens.

"We've got to help them, Lulu!"

"No, Fil, wait," said Lulu, holding Filbert by the tail.

Filbert looked on in disbelief as the donkey took the boy's net in his mouth and deftly scooped up a fleeing chicken. The hen thrashed about trying to free herself, but it was no use. The donkey held her high in the air, proudly showing off his prize.

The small boy crouched and sprang from the donkey's back. He sailed through the air like a diver with perfect form, his cape flapping behind him. He collided with another chicken and they tumbled to the ground in a mass of feathers and dust. They rolled to a stop and began to struggle, hand to wing. The hen gave him a kick, but soon the blond boy overpowered her and wrestled her into submission. "I got one!" shouted the boy triumphantly.

"Lulu!" pleaded Filbert.

"Just watch, Fil."

Ten big fat hens pounced on the small blond boy. They smothered him like a giant potato. Holding him tight, they stuffed his cape in his mouth, muffling his cry for help. The donkey, noticing his fallen comrade, moved to rescue him. As he approached the helpless boy, Gunther threw a watermelon from atop the chicken coop. The melon exploded when it hit the ground, spraying red fruit fragments in all directions. Trying to avoid the splatter, the donkey backed right into a hidden rope trap. Gunther shouted, "Now!" and the rope closed around the donkey's legs, hoisting him high in the air. The battle was over and the chickens were victorious!

"What's going on!?" exclaimed Cornelius emerging from his workshop.

"I'm not sure," said Filbert.

"Those are just my cousins, Fil. They always play around with the chickens," explained Lulu. "Let's go say hi."

Filbert, Cornelius, and Lulu had to wade through the cheering chickens to get to the donkey. Dangling upside-down from his hind legs, the donkey said, "Hey Lulu, Uncle Corn, how's it going?"

"Not too bad, Ryan. How's things with you?" asked Lulu.

"Ha! Not bad. I guess they were ready for us this time. Do you think you could cut me down? I'm getting a little dizzy."

Cornelius gave Gunther a signal; the rope and the donkey dropped to the ground with a *thud!* A moment later, the small boy was roughly deposited at Lulu's feet by several chickens. He was completely wrapped in his red cape and unable to move. The end was still stuffed in his mouth.

"MMMM, MMMM," the boy pleaded and wriggled, attempting to free himself. The chickens laughed. Lulu unraveled him and he quickly got to his feet.

"Ah ha!" The boy sprang into the air, leaping at the closest chicken, but the donkey caught him by the cape and held him aloft. He ran in place for several seconds before he finally

Donkey and the Tiniest Pig

tired out. "Put me down!" protested the boy. "I'll be good." The donkey spat him onto the ground.

"So this is the flying whale? Cool," said the donkey to Lulu.

Squirrel Trouble

The small boy walked up to Filbert and poked him several times. "Niiiice," he said. "A little squishy, but niiiice."

"Where are my manners? Filbert, this is Ryan and The Tiniest Pig. They're my nephews," said Cornelius.

"One of your nephews is a donkey?" asked Filbert.

"I'm not really a donkey. I was helping a warlock friend of mine with his spells and things got of hand," said Ryan.

"Oh, okay," said Filbert, completely baffled. "How long do you have to be a donkey for?"

"Well ... that hasn't been determined yet. Hopefully, he will be able to turn me back into myself before school starts."

"And your name is Tiniest Pig?" asked Filbert, turning to the little blond boy.

"*The* Tiniest Pig," corrected the boy. Then he made a rough noisy laughing sound that resembled a snort from a pig. "It's actually Liam, but Uncle Cornelius likes to call me that, for some reason. TP for short."

"By the way, what are you doing here, Filbert?" asked Cornelius.

"I came to talk to you about the inspection," answered Filbert.

"Fine, but can we talk after lunch?"

"Yes, sir."

"Lulu, can you get our guests something to eat? I still have lots of feathers to pluck for the next batch of scarves," said Cornelius.

"Okay," she replied. "I'm taking orders," she announced, and bolted for the house.

Donkey and the Tiniest Pig

At the back door, Lulu started giving instructions. "Filbert, set four places at the picnic table. Ryan, TP, follow me."

Filbert had just finished setting the table when the back door flew open. The Tiniest Pig stormed out, stopped, and turned back toward the door with a scowl on his face. "Get it yourself!" he yelled, red-faced. Then he stomped off around the front of the house.

Lulu and Ryan appeared in the doorway. "I should have said please, I guess?" said Lulu.

"That's not it," said Ryan. "He really hates milk. He gets upset even at the mention of it."

"Why?" asked Filbert, in disbelief.

"I can't say for sure. It's been this way ever since his class went on a field trip to a dairy farm. Apparently he got into some sort of an argument with a cow," explained Ryan.

"Something you might have warned me about before we started working in the kitchen," said Lulu. "What should we do?"

"Whatever you do, don't say *milk*," answered Ryan.

The three of them went after TP and found him sitting on the ground, his cape pulled up over his head.

"TP, I'm sorry that I told you to get the mmm ...," said Lulu.

"The M-word," whispered Ryan.

"Yeah, the M-word. Sorry about that," she said, but he refused to acknowledge her.

"Come on, TP, this is stupid. Lulu didn't know that you hate the M-word," said Ryan.

"Why don't you like milk?" blurted out Filbert.

"Filbert!" exclaimed Ryan and Lulu in unison.

Squirrel Trouble

The Tiniest Pig let out a growl, jumped up, and ran off. Ryan chased after him. Lulu dashed into the house, returning moments later with a peanut butter sandwich. The boy came at them, grunting and growling. They threw the sandwich toward the backyard. The Tiniest Pig pounced on it like a cat. After eating, he curled up in a ball and slept in a bed of flowers.

"He was just hungry and tired," said Ryan. "He's 5."

"Okay, lunchtime," said Lulu. When they got back to the picnic table, there were four hens sitting there with napkins tied around their necks, holding forks and knives. Lulu shooed them off. She and Ryan went back into the kitchen and returned with lunch.

After they ate and cleaned up, The Tiniest Pig came wandering over. "I just wanted to say sorry about earlier," he said. "I feel better now. Can I have ice cream?"

"You like ice cream?" asked Filbert.

"I love ice cream!" said TP, clapping his hands excitedly.

"But it comes from ..."

"Nooo, Fil!" shouted Lulu. "Ice cream is ice cream, let's leave it at that."

Cornelius returned from his workshop covered in chicken feathers.

"You sure spend a lot of time plucking feathers off of chickens," said The Tiniest Pig.

"Well, TP, when you own a business that makes scarves out of chicken feathers, that's just what you do," replied Cornelius. "Okay, Filbert. Tell me what's on your mind."

Donkey and the Tiniest Pig

Filbert thought for a moment and then he said, "Why do you call your nephew The Tiniest Pig?"

"Heh heh," chuckled Cornelius. "Years ago, when Liam — that's his real name — was even smaller than he is now, his favorite story was The Three Little Pigs and he made me read it to him over and over again. I just started calling him The Tiniest Pig and it stuck."

"Oh, okay. So just to be clear, he's not called The Tiniest Pig because he smells like feet or poop, right?"

"No, Filbert. Wasn't there something else you wanted to talk about?"

"Is the inspection going to hurt?" blurted Filbert.

"It's not going to hurt. Why do you think that?"

"Well, Lulu said that they were going to scrape my skin off, and my brother said that they would poke me with needles, and I was dreaming that they put me in a cage, and Snarlfoot, and my Dad, and my Mom, and ..."

"Whoa, whoa. Hold on there, Filbert. It's not going to be like that. They're not going to hurt you. Most likely, they'll just look at you and ask us a few questions about how you behave around people. They just want to be sure that you're not going to hurt anyone."

"Are you sure?" asked Filbert.

"Yes. I'll be with you the entire time and I won't let them hurt you. I promise."

Filbert felt much better.

"There is one thing you have to understand, Fil. In the eyes of The City, I'm responsible for you. If you get caught flying

Squirrel Trouble

around without a license, The City might fine me, or worse."

"What's worse than a fine?"

"Well, if they see you as dangerous, it's possible that I could go to jail. So please be careful."

"I will," promised Filbert.

"What's this?" asked Cornelius, pointing to a large white pick-up truck pulling into the front yard. A tiny black-and-white penguin hopped out of the driver's side. Cornelius went over to see what it wanted. They talked for a bit, the penguin handed Cornelius a business card, got back in the truck, and drove away.

"What did he want?" asked Filbert.

"He's the leader of a crew of penguins who do odd jobs and was wondering if I had any work for them. I think his name was Ross."

"I don't think you should hire them," said Filbert soberly. "My Dad says that penguins have ice for brains."

"Thanks for the warning, Fil. Have a good trip home and we'll see you on Tuesday."

"Bye, Cornelius," said Filbert, taking to the sky.

CHAPTER 4

Salamanders in the Park

On Tuesday, Filbert was finishing up his chores when Edweena came to ask him to drag the clams.

"Can't Roger do it? I have to go to the inspection," said Filbert.

"He's already gone off to Ollie's Gardens with some of the other kids," said Edweena.

"Oh, sea sponge!"

"Watch your language."

Filbert took the clams to Salt Water Park, where most of Deep End's residents brought their pets. It was a big open sandy area. Smeepy and Smarple saw a pack of clams and bounded over to them. They all yipped and yapped greetings to each other. One of the clams scooped up a bunch of sand and started to gargle loudly; the others did the same.

Squirrel Trouble

"Stop that," said Filbert. "I didn't bring you here to gargle. You have to do your business so I can take you back home!"

Smeepy and Smarple continued to gargle along with the others, ignoring Filbert. Leashing them up, he dragged them away from the group. Urgently, he pled with them to do their business. The clams stared longingly at their gargling friends.

"Poop already!" shouted Filbert. "I have places to go."

Still there was no reaction from Smeepy or Smarple.

"Please poop!" pleaded Filbert. Bribery, he thought. "If you poop now, I'll bring you some Fishy Fingers when I come home tonight."

Smeepy turned to Smarple and squeaked something in clam speech. Smarple returned the same sound and both of them promptly did their business. Filbert scooped it up in a sack and shuddered. "Gross!" Then they were on their way.

It was getting late. Filbert needed to get to Lulu's, pronto. At home he put Smeepy and Smarple in their clam house and rushed to the surface of the water. Filbert burst from the ocean at full speed. A huge geyser shot into the air, glittering in the sun as it cascaded back down.

"WOOHOO!" shouted Filbert. The chill of wind blowing on his wet skin never failed to thrill him. It felt like freedom. "YEE HAW!"

"Filbert!" called a voice from behind him.

Looking back, Filbert saw Snarlfoot the seagull, his wings pumping to catch up. He moved reasonably fast for being one of the oldest gulls around. He had a white head, gray wings, and black tail feathers. The feathers on his head

Salamanders in the Park

stuck out at odd angles, giving the impression that he was perpetually stressed out.

"Hey Snarly!" shouted Filbert.

"Where you heading?" asked the gull.

"On my way to Lulu's."

"She's your new human friend?"

"That's her."

"Mind if I come along?"

"Think you can keep up?"

"Keep up? I'm a bird!" Snarlfoot zoomed in beside Filbert, and then flew circles around him effortlessly. "Ha! I could show you a thing or two about flying, boy."

As they flew, Snarlfoot regaled Filbert with a story or two. After a bit, the seagull grew quiet and suddenly blurted out, "The crows be pecking at the STANK on me feet!"

"What crows?" asked Filbert, looking around. Then he remembered that Snarlfoot often shouted strange things for no apparent reason. Filbert's mom told him that was because his brains were rattled.

Snarlfoot yelled a couple of more crazy things before he snapped out of it. "Oh, hello Filbert," he said, as if they had just met. Filbert had to explain where they were going all over again. Snarlfoot apologized and said, "The old noggin isn't what is used to be."

As they approached The City, Filbert realized that there wasn't time to fly above the clouds to stay hidden. They would just have to risk being spotted. At their speed not a lot of people noticed them anyway. The few who did only had

Squirrel Trouble

time to point and stare before Filbert and Snarlfoot zipped out of sight.

By the time they reached Dirty Dog Park, it was eerily quiet. Filbert hoped the squirrels wouldn't notice him. Going around the park to get to Lulu's would take a lot longer.

Filbert and Snarlfoot glided quietly over the trees and grass. Suddenly, flashing lights and sirens started going off all over the park. "Destroyer!" someone yelled.

FFFFIP! ZIP! THIP! Something whizzed past them.

"They're shooting acorns at us!" said Snarlfoot.

PAP! THUD! POP! "Ha Ha! They don't hurt," said Filbert, as the acorn artillery found its mark.

"UUFF!" One hit Snarlfoot in the stomach. "Speak for yourself, you big brute!"

"Get behind me," said Filbert. Snarlfoot landed on Filbert's back and held on tight.

After several more direct hits the acorns stopped coming.

"They gave up," said Filbert.

"Silly little furballs. They're probably peeing in their pants," said Snarlfoot.

"Squirrels don't wear pants, Snarly. Some of them have nice jackets, though."

Up ahead, the branches of a tree spread apart, revealing a curious sight. There were squirrels pulling back on a piece of rubber. Some kind of creature that Filbert had never seen before was holding onto it. The squirrels let go and the creature came flying at Filbert. *WHOOOSH!* It zipped by, nearly hitting Filbert in the face.

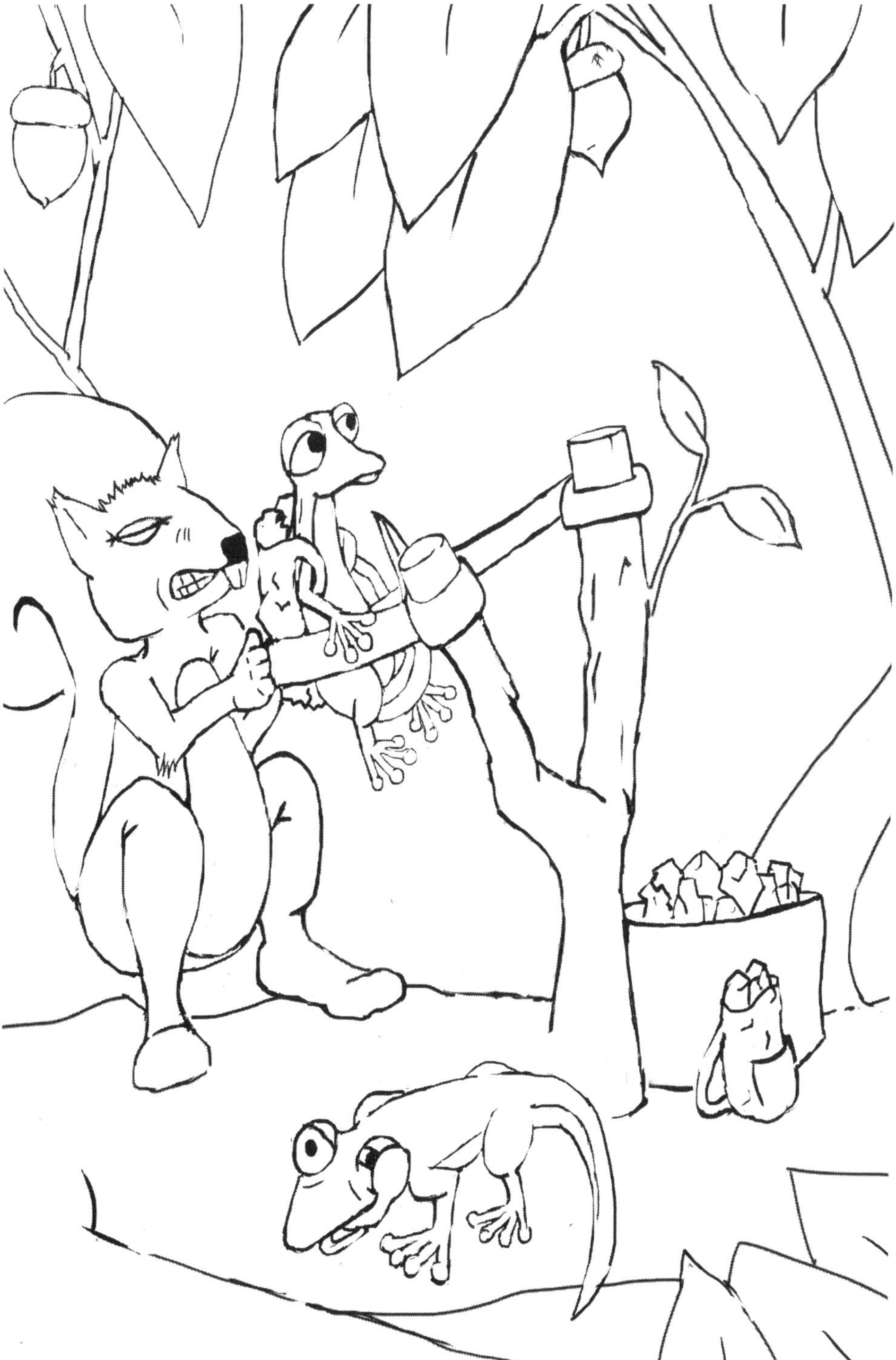

Squirrel Trouble

"What was that?" asked Snarlfoot. *FFFOOSH! SWWIIFF! SWAFFLE!* Several more of the black-and-yellow-spotted creatures flew by. Branches were parting all over the park, and behind each gap in the trees was a crew of squirrels. They all had pieces of rubber stretched between two sticks and a line of the mysterious creatures waiting to be loaded in and launched.

"AAAAA!" screamed a creature as it shot by.

WHAP! One hit Filbert square in the face and stuck there. It had a long snakelike body with four legs and it was wearing a backpack.

"They're shooting some kind of eels at us!"

"No, they're salamanders. Yuck!" said Snarlfoot. "They're amphibians, vile little things!"

All over the park, salamanders were being fired from the squirrel slingshots. *WHAP! WHAP! WHAP!* Three more salamanders found their mark, sticking to Filbert. *SPLURP!* Another one hit him at an angle and careened off, tumbling away end over end. The sky was dark with salamanders now.

"They're starting to weigh me down," said Filbert, alarmed.

"Not if I can help it!" yelled Snarlfoot. He started pecking at the closest salamander, poking him in the face and belly. It finally lost its grip and fell off. "Leave it to me, Fil."

"Hurry, I don't know how many more I can carry!"

The seagull darted from salamander to salamander, poking, kicking, and pecking. Snarlfoot had pried off 10 of the tenacious little beasts in no time at all.

Salamanders in the Park

"Keep pulling them off, Snarly!" shouted Filbert.

"Their backpacks are full of rocks," said Snarlfoot. As he scrambled to one side of Filbert, a salamander hit him right in the face, its sticky toes wrapped around his head. Snarlfoot stumbled and fell backward off of Filbert.

"Snarlfoot! Nooo!" yelled Filbert. More and more of the moist little projectiles were sticking to him. Slowly, he started to lose altitude. One of Filbert's eyes was covered by a salamander. Twisting and turning, Filbert writhed as hard as he could, but he could not shake them off. *SPLAT! SPLAT! SPLAT!* More of them stuck to him. He was so tired.

Filbert plummeted to the ground and slammed into the park with a loud *BOOM!* He tore through the grass, leaving a deep trench of mud in his wake.

Groggy from hitting the ground so hard, Filbert was not sure where he was. A horn sounded: *Do Dooo! Do Dooo!* Squirrels came streaming out of the bushes. They were cheering wildly.

"Yay, the Destroyer is down!"

"Hooray for squirrel justice!"

"Remember the Alamo!"

A large brown squirrel wearing a silver army helmet was shouting commands.

"Gets those ropes on that beast, quickly!"

Filbert could feel himself being dragged backward. Soon he was underneath the canopy of trees. More ropes were thrown over him. He tried to float, but he was securely tied down and unable to move at all.

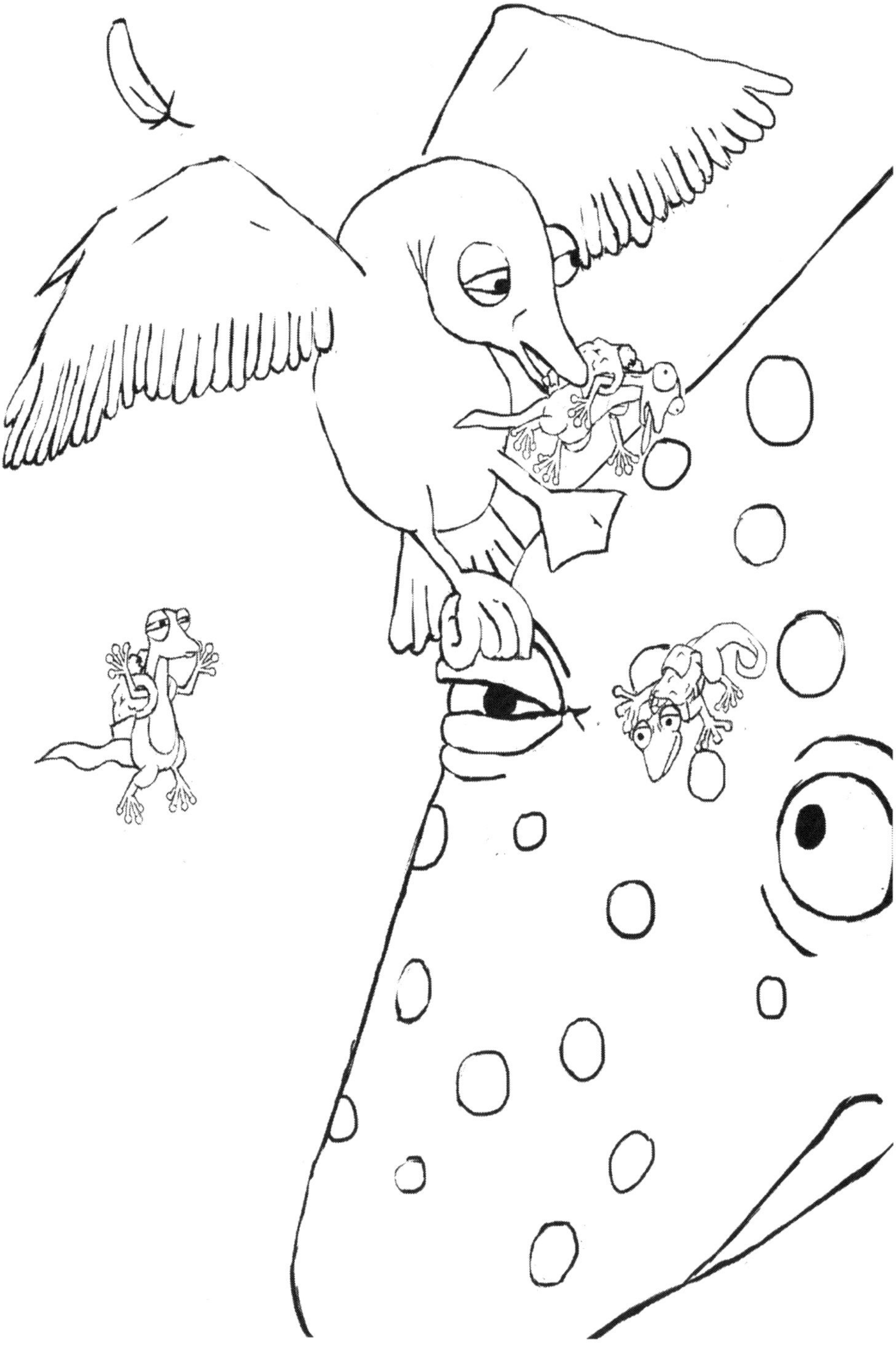

Salamanders in the Park

"Please, you have to let me go," pleaded Filbert. "I have to be somewhere."

"Boo!" yelled the crowd.

"Be quiet, Destroyer, or I'll have you gagged," warned the silver-helmeted squirrel.

"But I just—" Before he could finish speaking, a group of squirrels stuffed a giant sock in Filbert's mouth. Helpless, he watched as the squirrels swarmed around him. Many of them seemed to be building something. Still woozy from the crash, Filbert started to lose consciousness. His last thought before he blacked out was that he would never make the inspection now.

CHAPTER 5

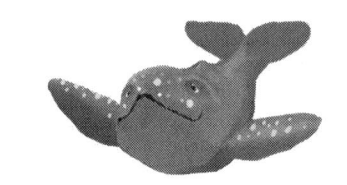

Crimes Against Furmanity

Filbert awoke to the sound of squeaky voices.

"Wake up, Destroyer."

Filbert was still unable to move and his mouth was very dry, but at least the sock had been removed and the salamanders were gone. He was inside now, yet he hadn't moved an inch. The ground was the same, but four walls and a ceiling had been erected around him. Hundreds of squirrels were sitting on benches to his left and right. Directly in front of him was a platform with a big empty chair on it.

"Destroyer! Down here! Hello!" said a small brown-and-white-spotted squirrel. He was wearing glasses and holding a tiny clipboard. "My name's Garrett. I'm your squirrel liaison for these proceedings."

Crimes Against Furmanity

"Proceedings?"

"You're here to face the charges against you."

"What?"

"You have to answer for your crimes against Furmanity."

"Furmanity?" said Filbert, confused.

"Furmanity is us. It's the population of squirrels here in the park."

Garrett explained what was going to take place with a grim but cute expression on his face. Filbert was charged with two crimes: destruction of the squirrel soccer stadium and the candy bombing of their swim meet. Filbert would have a chance to explain himself and then Commissioner Tiny Fingers, the leader of the squirrels, would decide whether he was guilty or innocent. If he was found guilty, he would be punished.

Filbert told Garrett that he didn't mean to do any of those things. He begged to be let go so he could make it to his licensing inspection. Garrett said that was impossible. A great feeling of dread washed over Filbert.

A horn sounded. The large brown squirrel with the silver helmet scurried down a tree and in through a hole in the roof. He stood next to the empty chair.

"General Knothole, commander of the Armed Squirrel Forces," announced a fat squirrel. The crowd cheered.

Next, a tall, thin gray squirrel with a long silver beard slowly climbed down the same tree and sat in the empty chair.

"Commissioner Tiny Fingers! Leader of the Free Squirrels!" boomed the announcer.

Squirrel Trouble

The crowd went wild. They cheered and threw acorns at Filbert. Tears welled up in his eyes.

"Everyone, be seated," said the commissioner, quieting the crowd. "Let's get started. Councilor Garrett, please proceed."

Garrett started by describing the two offenses that Filbert was accused of committing. Next, several witnesses were brought in to attest to the validity of the charges. The crowd was very upset and had to be hushed on several occasions. As each witness described the terrible things that had happened to them, the sense of dread that Filbert felt grew thicker and more real. After the final witness had testified, the Commissioner rose from his chair.

"Destroyer, do you have anything to say in your defense?"

Filbert leaned over and whispered in Garrett's ear. "The Destroy — um — defendant wishes to be addressed as Filbert," stated Garrett with a smirk. The crowd burst out laughing. Commissioner Tiny Fingers fell to his knees cackling like a deranged fruit bat. General Knothole tried to help him up, but was so overcome with mirth that he and the Commissioner ended up on the ground. There were several minutes of uncontrolled guffawing.

"If he did not wish to be called Destroyer, he should not have done so much destroying," replied the Commissioner. "Now, does the Destroyer have anything to say in his defense?"

"I didn't mean for any of this to happen. It wasn't my fault!" pled Filbert. "I didn't know that you had a soccer stadium in the bush I landed in." Boos and hisses rose from the crowd. "The candy was supposed to be a gift, not an attack!" The squirrels grew angrier with each excuse Filbert made. "Please, it's not my fault," continued Filbert.

At the end of Filbert's plea, the Commissioner and General Knothole scampered up the tree to confer in private. Most of the audience filed out of the courtroom. Outside, Filbert could see that popcorn and soda were being sold.

"Do you think they will let me go?" Filbert asked.

"Well, I can't say for sure, but I'm convinced. If it was up to me, I would let you off," said Garrett.

"Thanks for being on my side."

Slowly the crowd worked its way back inside and sat down. The courtroom was silent in anticipation. The Commissioner rose from his chair to address the crowd.

"It is the opinion of General Knothole and myself that the Destroyer did not intentionally cause the damage and mayhem that resulted from his actions."

A glimmer of hope sparked in Filbert.

"Nooo!" shrieked someone in the back. An angry murmur spread through the courtroom.

"Boo!"

"Hiss!"

Filbert thought that just maybe he was going to make it to Cornelius's house in time.

"Quiet down!" roared the Commissioner. "Although he did not intend to cause such damage, the Destroyer must be held responsible for his actions."

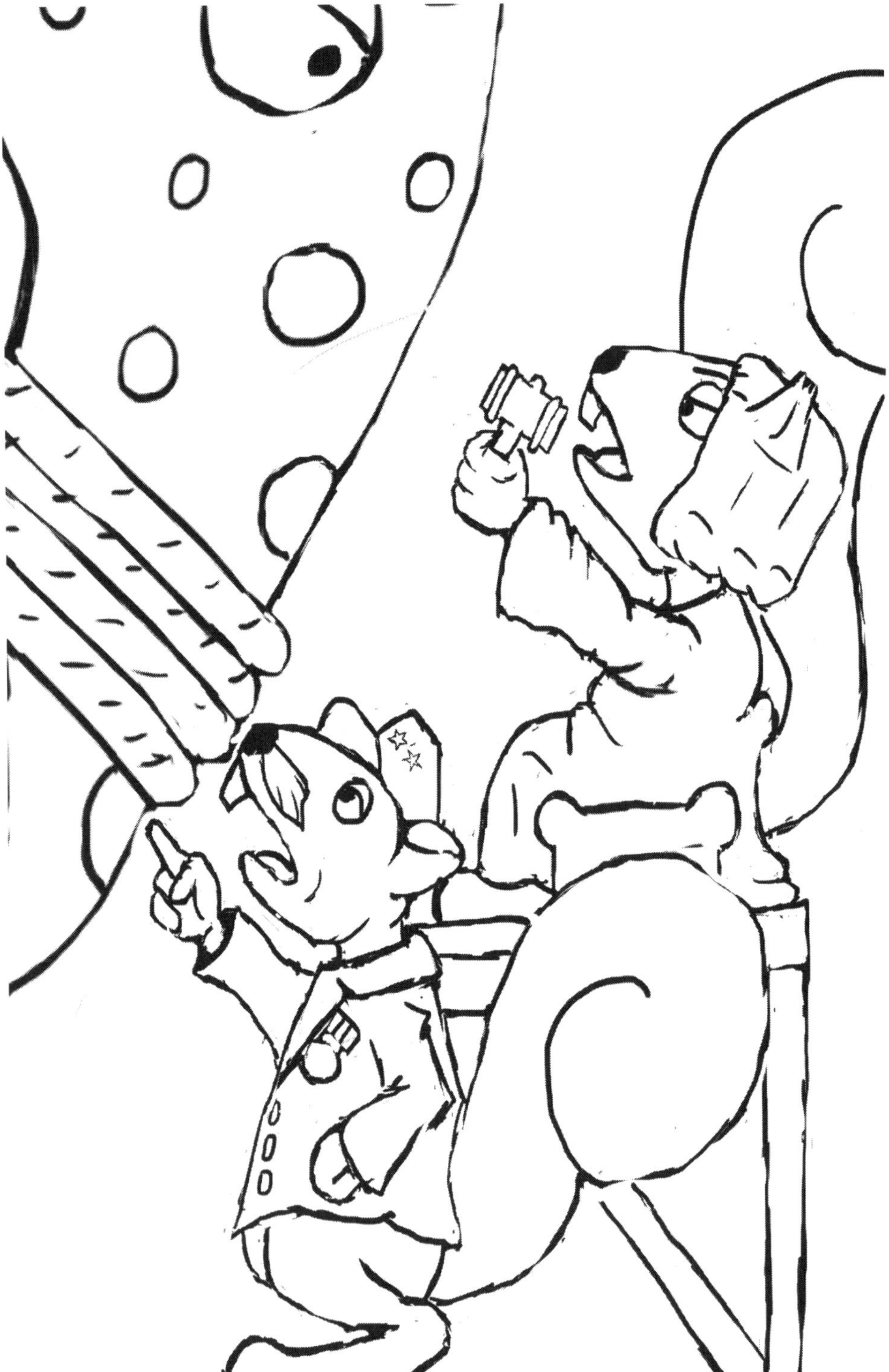

Crimes Against Furmanity

The spark of hope was quickly extinguished by these words.

"I hereby sentence the Destroyer to three hours of Furmmunity service!" exclaimed the Commissioner.

The squirrels erupted with joy, applauding and shouting.

"Yay!"

"Woohoo!"

"Justice!"

Three hours, screamed Filbert in his head. His heart sank. There was no way that he could get to the inspection in time. Now he would never be allowed to move around freely on land.

"If I may, Commissioner?" said Garrett. "What will be required of my client during these hours of service?"

"He shall make party hats for every squirrel in the park!"

The crowd broke into a chant: "Par-tee hats, par-tee hats!"

"I'm sorry, Filbert. It doesn't look like you will be able to make your appointment," said Garret. "I'll stick around and help you make the hats, if you like."

"Thanks," whispered Filbert, deflated.

Filbert accepted his punishment in silence. Construction paper was brought to him and his fins were untied. Hoping nobody would notice, he turned from the crowd and brushed away a tear. With some instruction from Garrett, it wasn't long before Filbert was churning out hats.

A line of squirrels stretched out in front of him. At first they were very rude. They called him "stinky" and were critical of the hats he made. Garrett admonished the rude squirrels, but the insults continued.

Squirrel Trouble

Then something unexpected happened. A young squirrel, no bigger than two acorns tied together, said, "Thank you, Destroyer. This is a fine party hat."

Surprised by the thanks, Filbert said, "Um, you're welcome, squirrel."

From that moment on, the insults ceased. Filbert's spirits were lifted slightly. He and Garrett chatted while they worked. Filbert felt useful and industrious. He was providing a service; he took pride in the hats he made.

As the line began to dwindle, Filbert started to think about what might happen to Cornelius if he missed the inspection. The dread was creeping back over him like a storm cloud.

Once the final squirrel had his hat, Filbert urgently asked, "Commissioner, are we even now?"

"Yes, I think that officially makes you and the Free Squirrel Nation even," declared Commissioner Tiny Fingers. "Release the Destroyer!" The roof began to retract at a signal from the Commissioner. "You are free to go."

"I won't ever bother you again," said Filbert sadly. Looking over at Garrett, he said, "You're a good squirrel. Thanks for your help." Filbert flew away as fast as he could.

CHAPTER 6

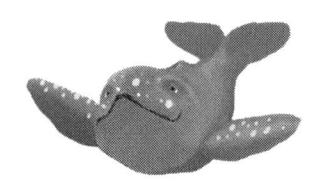

Taking Responsibility

Hoping that he could somehow still make it in time, Filbert streaked through the sky like a missile. He was just a gray blur when he hit the ground in Lulu's back yard. *KABOOM!* Filbert lay there panting as chickens streamed out of the hen house to see what was happening.

Catching his breath, Filbert said, "Did I make it in time?"

"Make what?" asked a hen.

"Did you make us something?" asked a second hen. "Is it a cake?"

At the mention of cake, the chickens became excited and started clucking.

"What are you talking about? Where's Cornelius?"

"Where's our cake?"

"There's no cake," said Filbert, curtly.

Squirrel Trouble

The chickens groaned disappointedly and began to wander away. No one knew where Cornelius, Lulu, or Gunther were.

"They must have been arrested," moaned Filbert. "It's all my fault."

Like a wildfire, panic spread throughout the yard.

"We're doomed!"

"Who's going to feed us?"

It was a full-blown riot! Chickens ran around like their heads were cut off, screaming and yapping. Rocks and bottles were being thrown; hens were trying to get into the main house. A group of fowl surrounded Filbert and started throwing rocks and mud at him.

"Soap on a rope! What's going on out here?" shouted Cornelius. Gunther and Lulu were with him. It took about half an hour, but they finally got the chickens to calm down.

"Nobody's been arrested," announced Gunther. "Please, go back to your coop."

"Where have you been?" asked Filbert.

"We went to the supermarket. Where were you?"

"The stupid squirrels captured me."

Lulu brought out hot chocolate and offered a cup to Filbert.

Filbert told his story as he slurped at the warm beverage. Lulu was very sad and gave him a big hug.

"So what happened when the inspector showed up?" asked Filbert.

"I told him that I thought the appointment was for next week and that you were at the groomer's getting your tail waxed,"

Taking Responsibility

said Cornelius. "He wasn't very happy, but he rescheduled."

"Yay!" exclaimed Filbert.

"It's not as good as it sounds. If you don't pass that inspection next week, they'll revoke my license to keep the chickens."

"Why? What do they have to do with it?" protested Filbert.

"If I have an unlicensed and possibly harmful animal, The City can't grant me a license for other animals. My business depends on you passing that inspection. I think you should probably spend the night before with us, just to be safe."

"I'll ask my parents."

On his way back home, Filbert found Snarlfoot sitting on buoy 159.

"Hey, Snarly!" said Filbert. "Wow, I'm glad you're okay. What happened after you got hit by that salamander?"

"Well, I shook him off and was getting ready to fly back to help you when a gang of squirrels jumped me. They tied my wings behind my back and hung a sign on me that said I smelled like feet. They told me to leave and if they caught me again they would do terrible things to me with acorns."

"Awful."

"It took hours to walk home. What happened with you?"

After hearing Filbert's story, Snarlfoot offered to help him get revenge on those "furry pirates." Filbert said that he was done with them and needed to get home.

At home Filbert found his mother working in the urchin patch.

"Hi, honey. How did the inspection go?"

Squirrel Trouble

"Not so good."

"What happened?"

Filbert explained about Snarlfoot, the salamanders, and the squirrels and how he had missed the inspection.

"Oh, my poor sweet little seahorse. I knew that it wasn't safe to let you go all by yourself! Come here and give me a hug," said mother. "Snarlfoot has one thing right. You can't trust amphibians. As far as I'm concerned, you either breathe water or air, not both."

Edweena took Filbert inside, gave him some nice cool sponges to put on his eyes, and sent him to rest in bed.

That evening, Roger came home.

"I'm sorry everything went so wrong," said Roger.

"Thanks. It's okay, though. I'll pass next week's appointment."

Roger had a look on his face like he just ate a stinging jellyfish.

"What?" asked Filbert.

"Mom and Dad said that it was too dangerous for you to visit Lulu anymore."

"That's crazy! I have to go back or Cornelius will lose his business!" Filbert shot out of bed and rushed downstairs.

Filbert confronted his parents. He pleaded, bargained, and threatened. He even squealed like a narwhal caught in an elevator shaft, but in the end Edweena and Richard stood firm.

"Look here, boy. I'm sorry that your friend might lose his job, but our concern is your safety. I don't want to hear any more about it," said Dad sternly.

Taking Responsibility

Filbert was seething. He went right to sleep without a word to his parents. All night long he had terrible nightmares, dreaming that Lulu and Cornelius were put in jail and that the chickens all lost their homes and had to wander the streets, begging for worms and toilet paper. Poor Gunther had to take a job at a local shoe store, where he was forced to smell very large and sweaty feet.

For the next few days, Filbert moped around. He was sluggish and surly, refusing to speak to anyone. Not even Smeepy and Smarple could rouse him from his melancholy. When Edweena came to tuck him in at night, he turned away as she went to kiss him. It made him feel empty when he refused love from his mother, but he didn't know how else to act.

One night, about the time that Edweena usually came in to say goodnight, the boys' father showed up instead. He tucked Roger in and turned to Filbert.

"That's it! I've had enough of this. Tomorrow, you will get up, have breakfast, drag the clams, and go to Whale Song. Do you hear me?" asked Dad.

"Mm uh," muttered Filbert.

"Look at me, boy. Do you understand me?"

"Yes, sir," said Filbert, grudgingly.

"Good."

After Dad left the room, Roger said, "Don't you love us anymore, Filbert?"

His brother's question struck him right in the heart. Filbert cried as quietly as he could, but knew Roger could hear him anyway. Roger went to Filbert's bed, hugged him, and said, "Don't be sad, Filbert."

"I still love you and Mom ... and Dad too," blurted Filbert. "But I promised Cornelius that I would be there. He risked everything for me. How can I let him down?"

"It's not your fault. There's nothing you can do about it."

Something clicked in Filbert's head.

"I have to go. Mom and Dad always say that I should take responsibility for myself. Even the stupid squirrels said it."

"What are you going to do?"

"Tomorrow I'm going to get up, eat breakfast, and we're going to take the clams for a drag. I'm not coming home from that drag. I'm going to Lulu's!"

The next morning, Filbert woke up to find his brother staring at him.

"Are you really going to run away today?" asked Roger fearfully.

Filbert knew from experience that Roger wasn't going to be able to keep quiet. Thinking quickly, he said, "No way! After thinking about it, I decided that Mom and Dad would be too angry."

He could see the fear drain out of his brother as Roger took a deep breath. "I'm so glad you're not going, Filbert. You know, I was going to tell on you."

"Really? I had no idea."

Downstairs at breakfast, Filbert had trouble eating. A big ball of dread was churning in his stomach. The fear of losing

Taking Responsibility

his parents' love made his heart ache, but he couldn't let Cornelius, Lulu, and the chickens down.

Once breakfast was over, on his way out the door, Filbert kissed Edweena and said, "I love you, Mom." Roger was already waiting for him with the clams all leashed up. Filbert went to say hi to Smeepy and Smarple, but they ignored him. When he tried to pet them, Smeepy jumped up and nipped at his fins.

"Ouch!" shouted Filbert. "What's wrong with you two?"

"Ha! See, they don't like you more than me," taunted Roger.

At Salt Water Park, Smeepy and Smarple rushed over to a large group of clams who were already busy gargling and swaying back and forth.

"Oh man! We're going to be here all day," said Filbert. "Can you go get them, Roger?"

As Roger headed toward the clams, Filbert knew that was his chance. He was scared but determined to go. No matter what happened to him, he couldn't let his friends down.

CHAPTER 7

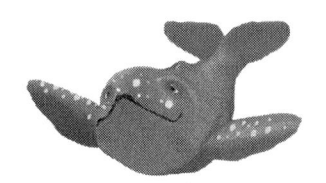

Sneaking Away

On his way to Cornelius's, Filbert decided not to mention that he had been forbidden to come. He suspected that Cornelius, being a father, would send him back to his parents even if it meant that he would be in trouble with The City. When he landed in front of the chicken coop, Gunther was there to greet him. They talked a bit and then Gunther went off to announce Filbert's arrival. A few moments later, the rooster returned with Cornelius in tow.

"Ah, Filbert, it's good to see you," said Cornelius.

"Thank you, sir. It's good to be here."

"How are your parents doing?"

"What?" asked Filbert nervously.

"With all the trouble you've had lately, I mean. I would be very concerned if it was Lulu going off somewhere by herself."

Sneaking Away

"Ah ... no, they, um, are fine with it," stuttered Filbert.

"Well, I'm glad that they trust you so much. Trust is a delicate thing. It takes a long time to build up, but only one mistake to totally destroy it."

"Yes, sir. What are you working on?" said Filbert, feeling a little weird inside.

"A lotion for the chickens!" exclaimed Cornelius, his eyes brightened. "It kind of numbs them and at the same time it speeds up the new feather growth. It's made from aloe and banana slug slime."

"What?"

"Don't ask me why, but it works great! The only problem is that it stinks like steamy gorilla breath."

Lulu came out of the house and said hello to Filbert.

"Okay, you two. I've got to get back to work. Try to stay out of trouble," said Cornelius.

Filbert's secret was screaming to be told. Unable to hold it in any longer, he blurted it to Lulu and felt immediate relief. It was just like letting out a giant burp, it felt so good.

"Filbert! How could you?" asked Lulu accusingly. "You lied to your parents and ran away!"

"I had no choice. I couldn't let your dad lose his business."

"What are you going to do?"

"First, I'm going to pass that inspection. After that ... I don't know."

"We can't tell Gunther, he'll go right to Daddy. Maybe Ryan could help us figure out what to do," said Lulu. "We can go to his house in the morning."

Squirrel Trouble

"You mean the donkey? How could he help?"

"He wore a cat on his head for a whole day, after his parents told him not to," explained Lulu.

Filbert stared at her blankly; he had no idea what she was talking about.

"His parents were super mad at him, but somehow he talked them out of punishing him."

"I don't know, Lulu. What if your dad finds out?"

"He'll be working all morning. We'll only be gone for a little while."

"Okay, but how are we going to keep people from seeing me?"

"I got an idea for that," said Lulu with a proud grin. "Me and some of the hens have been working on it for days now."

"What is it?"

"It's a secret. I'll show it to you tomorrow."

Filbert spent the rest of the day trying to forget how angry his parents were going to be with him. When night finally came, he settled down on Cornelius's roof to sleep. Once again, his slumber was plagued with nightmares.

Filbert woke with the fear that his parents didn't love him anymore. Part of him wanted to rush home and beg their forgiveness, but it was too late.

At breakfast, Filbert soaked in an enormous tub of salt water that Cornelius had made especially for him. They ate in the yard because Filbert was too large to fit in the house.

"Wow! This is the life," said Filbert, chowing down on pancakes and corn fritters.

Sneaking Away

"I'll be working in my shop until about noon. The inspector is coming around 12:30, so we can have lunch together before he arrives."

"Okay, Daddy. We'll be playing around the house," said Lulu. She turned to Filbert and gave him a wink. Filbert winked back.

"Is there something in your eye, Filbert?" asked Cornelius.

"Umm, uh ... I ..." stammered Filbert.

"Don't worry, Daddy, I'll flush it out for him," said Lulu, quickly ushering Filbert away. "That was close. Don't be so obvious, Fil."

"Sorry."

Lulu led Filbert around the back of the two-story hen house, past Cornelius's workshop, and into a stand of trees. She whistled three times and made a sound like she was hocking up snot. *Whorrrk! Whorrk! Whorrk!*

"Gross!" said Filbert.

From somewhere in the shadows came a hissing and two quick bird calls. "*SSSSSSSS. Cawcaw. Cawcaw.*"

"There's the counter-signal," she said.

Back into the trees and bushes they went. There was a small clearing where several hens were busily working on a large covered wagon. It was about 10 feet tall and 15 feet long with four wheels. There was a place to sit and steer up in the front. Filbert noticed there was something not right about this wagon. It wasn't a wagon at all! It was only a cardboard box painted to look like one.

"What are you going to do with that?" asked Filbert.

Squirrel Trouble

"Put you inside," said Lulu.

"Awesome! Are you sure you can trust these chickens not to tell?"

"Yeah, Fil. Don't worry. Look who's in charge," said Lulu, pointing to a red hen coming around the back side of the wagon.

"Rita!" exclaimed Filbert.

Rita ran up to Filbert and gave him a giant hug. "My hens and I won't say a word. I still owe you for saving me from that mean old hawk. Plus, Lulu supplies all the worms we want for keeping our beaks shut," assured Rita with a wink.

"The worms have been dropped in the agreed-upon location. You can pick them up at any time," said Lulu. "Be sure you're not followed."

"No problem. We're like the wind, no one sees us coming or going," said Rita. The other chickens made blowing sounds and swayed in unison, illustrating Rita's point. "The wagon is all yours."

"Thank you," said Lulu, shaking Rita's extended wing.

Lulu opened the back of the wagon and motioned for Filbert to get in. He fit perfectly inside with a couple of feet to spare. When the doors were shut the box became dark except for the eye holes cut in the front where the sunlight poured in. Filbert pushed his face up against the front of the wagon; he could see reasonably well, at least what was in front of him. Lulu came into view and climbed up on the bench seat that was built into the top front of the wagon.

"Okay, Fil, just give it a shove and we're off."

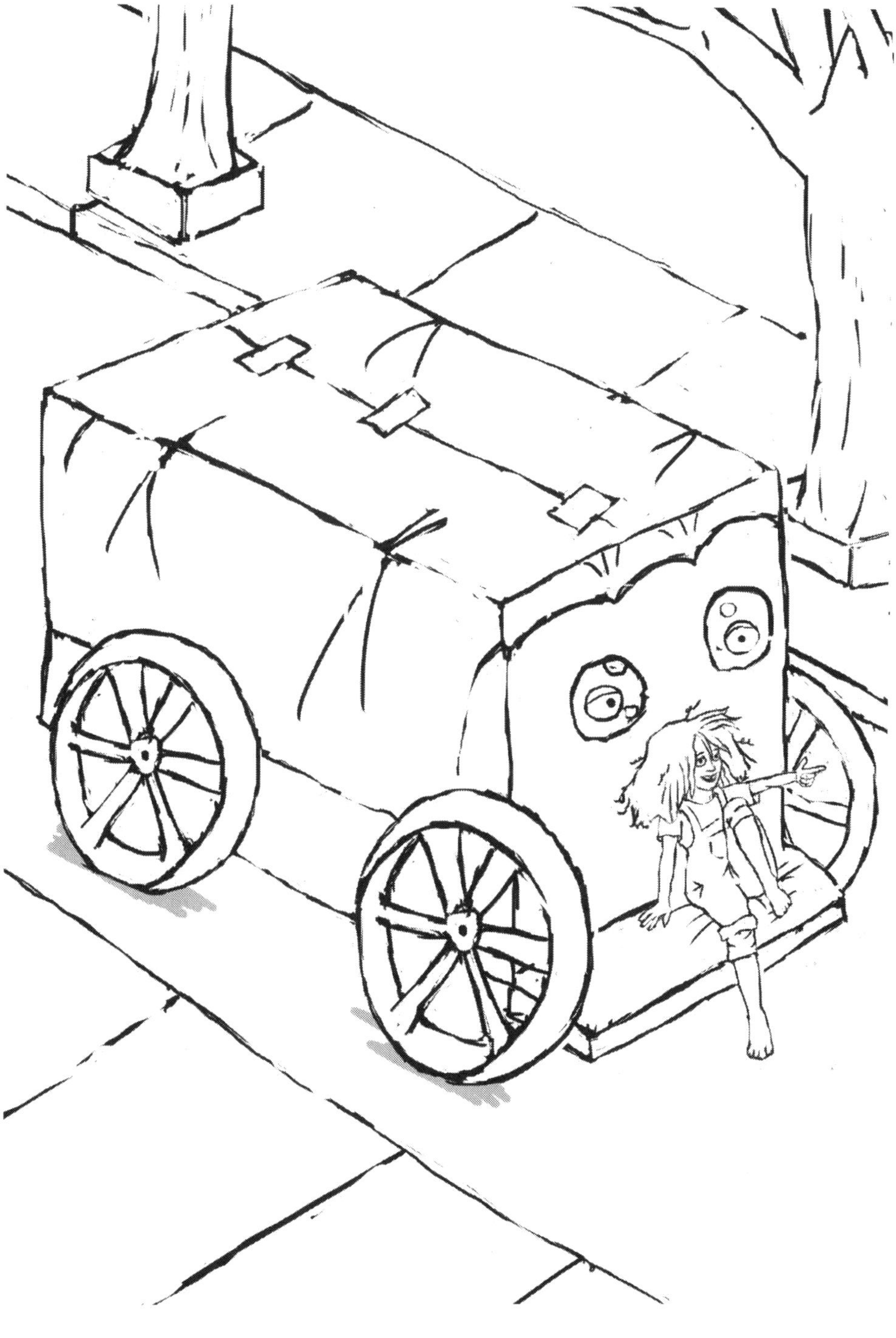

CHAPTER 8

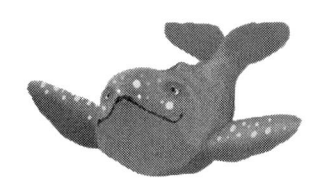

Penguins, Milk, And Fire

They slid along the street for a while, Lulu shouting directions. Filbert noticed that they were getting some astonished looks from people as they approached, but once they saw Lulu on the top of the wagon no one seemed to think much of it.

They came to a square house in the middle of the block.

"Pull over here, Fil," instructed Lulu quietly. "Just park it on the lawn while I go in and get Ryan."

Filbert waited for what seemed like forever. Lulu finally emerged from the house and climbed back onto the wagon.

"Where have you been?" asked Filbert. "I've been sitting out here like an oyster in a bathing suit."

"Sorry, Fil. Auntie Grazelda made me sit and talk with her.

Ryan and The Tiniest Pig went to pick up some okra and kiwi at the shopping center."

Pushing a wagon along the street, even one made of cardboard, was much slower than flying. It drove Filbert crazy. As they approached the parking lot, Filbert noticed Dirty Dog Park just across the street.

"I can't go over there," said Filbert.

"Don't be silly. Those smelly squirrels will never know you're here."

They pulled into a parking spot in front of Dawn's Specialty Meat Company. Ryan and The Tiniest Pig were there. TP was riding the coin-operated toy rocket ship. Filbert could hear TP saying he wanted to ride again. Ryan was telling him he'd already ridden it nine times.

"Ten is a good number," insisted The Tiniest Pig.

Lulu jumped down and explained to them about Filbert's predicament. She asked if they had any suggestions to fix it. The Tiniest Pig ran over to the wagon and kicked it.

"Cool! You in there, Fil?" he shouted.

"Quiet, you dirty little monkey," said Ryan. "If anybody knew he was in there, they'd call the police."

After discussing Filbert's problem, Ryan admitted he was stumped. "I'm not sure what to do, Fil."

"You can always join the circus," said TP.

"No one's joining the circus!" said Lulu firmly. "C'mon, guys. Fil needs our help."

After several minutes of brainstorming, the only idea they had involved an elaborate hoax in which Filbert had to fake his own death with a bulldozer and a handful of raisins.

"We're not getting anywhere. Let's take an ice cream break," said Lulu. She and the boys went into Tyler's Ice Cream and Ninja Emporium, leaving Filbert hidden in the wagon. A moment later, Filbert heard the familiar *clip-clop* of Ryan's hooves.

"What're you doing back so fast?" asked Filbert.

"They had a sign that said no shoes, no service," said Ryan sadly.

Lulu and The Tiniest Pig came back with two ice cream cones apiece. Lulu held Filbert's cone up to the eye slit in the wagon and with one tremendous *SLURP*, the cone disappeared.

"Take your cone, Ryan," said TP, munching away at his ice cream. *Sluurrp! Snort! Gorffle Gorffle!*

"With what hands?" asked Ryan sarcastically.

"Sorry." TP held the cone out to him.

Ryan proceeded to chomp away with his huge donkey teeth. *Glornk! Glornk! Glornk!*

"You two better slow down before you get brain freeze," warned Lulu.

"Too late," said TP. He fell to the ground and flopped around like a fish.

Suddenly, a loud commotion in the street caught Filbert's attention. A pick-up truck full of penguins was weaving erratically in and out of traffic. People were screaming and yelling, horns were blaring. *Honk! Honk!* But the crazed penguins paid them no mind. They continued to speed back

Penguins, Milk, And Fire

and forth along the street. The truck made a sharp turn, jumped the curb, and landed in the middle of the parking lot.

Eight enormous penguins spilled out of the truck. They were about nine feet tall and all black except for their white bellies. Filbert recognized the driver from Cornelius's house. He was less than two feet tall. They were staggering and wild-eyed; whooping and hollering, each of them took deep swigs off of a gallon of milk that was being passed around.

"Back up, there's no telling what they're capable of," said someone in the crowd.

"Thass riii! Y'all better clear out," slurred the miniature penguin, wiping milk from his beak with the back of his wing.

"Oh my gosh!" exclaimed Filbert. "Milk makes penguins crazy."

"MILK!" growled The Tiniest Pig, enraged. He ran off, calling, "G. O. A. T.S.! Goats, goats ... goats, goats!"

"Get them skyrockets, Lem," commanded the little penguin. "We're gonna have a little fun."

"Sure thing, Ross," said Lem. He scrambled up into the bed of the truck, retrieved several large fireworks, and set them in front of the little penguin.

Quickly, Ross handed each of his crew a skyrocket and began lighting the fuses. *Whoosh! Swhoosh! Voosh! Thoof!* They blasted into the air, raining sparks down on everyone below. The penguins cackled with delight as the fireworks exploded in brilliant colors. *Boom! Bang! Pow!* One rocket flew into the park and exploded in a tree. The tree burst into flames.

Squirrel Trouble

"Fire! Fire!"

The flames rapidly spread to the surrounding trees and bushes. Squirrels streamed out of their homes to safety.

"We have to help the squirrels," said Ryan.

"Not me," replied Filbert.

"That fire could consume the whole park!" shouted Lulu. "We've got to put it out!"

"Alright, I'll help," said Filbert, bursting out of the cardboard wagon.

"Oh no you don't," squeaked Ross. "That's our fire! No one's putting it out!"

Lulu, Ryan, and Filbert found themselves face to face with a line of huge, angry penguins.

"W-w-we don't want any trouble here," stuttered Lulu.

"Well, you got some now," shouted Ross. "Get them!" He was hopping up and down, egging on his crew, waving a giant pickle.

The penguins began to march forward emitting ominous beeping sounds. Before they could close in on Lulu and Filbert, Ryan dove into the middle of them. They surrounded him and wrestled Ryan to the ground. He didn't give up, though. Totally pinned down, Ryan shot snot rockets at his assailants.

"Don't forget the other two," shouted Ross.

As the penguins turned on Filbert and Lulu, a tiny voice rang out.

"Hold on there, you milk-drinking menaces!"

A herd of goats rumbled through the parking lot. Riding the lead goat was The Tiniest Pig, his cape flying in the wind.

Penguins, Milk, And Fire

They crashed into the line of penguins, sweeping them up as they stampeded through. Ross was frantically waving his pickle and squealing like an agonized yak. The Tiniest Pig's face was contorted into a battle sneer. He was yelling something, but it was drowned out by the bleating of the goats and the surprised shouts of the penguins.

"What in the world is going on?" asked Lulu. "Where did he get a herd of goats?"

"Don't ask. TP is a mystery," said Ryan, dragging himself free of the mayhem.

The rush of goats had done the trick! After being trampled, the penguins were scattered and dazed. Ryan and Lulu jumped on the nearest penguin and held him down. The crowd helped restrain the rest of the black-and-white troublemakers.

The fire still raging, Filbert sprang into action. He flew to the lake in the park, scooped up as much water as his mouth could hold, and sprayed it on the flames. He did this repeatedly, from lake to burning trees and back again. Filbert was exhausted by the time the fire department arrived, but his valiant effort managed to keep the blaze from spreading out of control.

The fire was just about out when the police showed up. They arrested the penguins and promptly threw a net over Filbert. As he was being hauled away, Filbert could hear the crowd protesting his arrest, but the police were adamant.

"The whale is going downtown. There's a warrant out for his arrest," said the officer in charge.

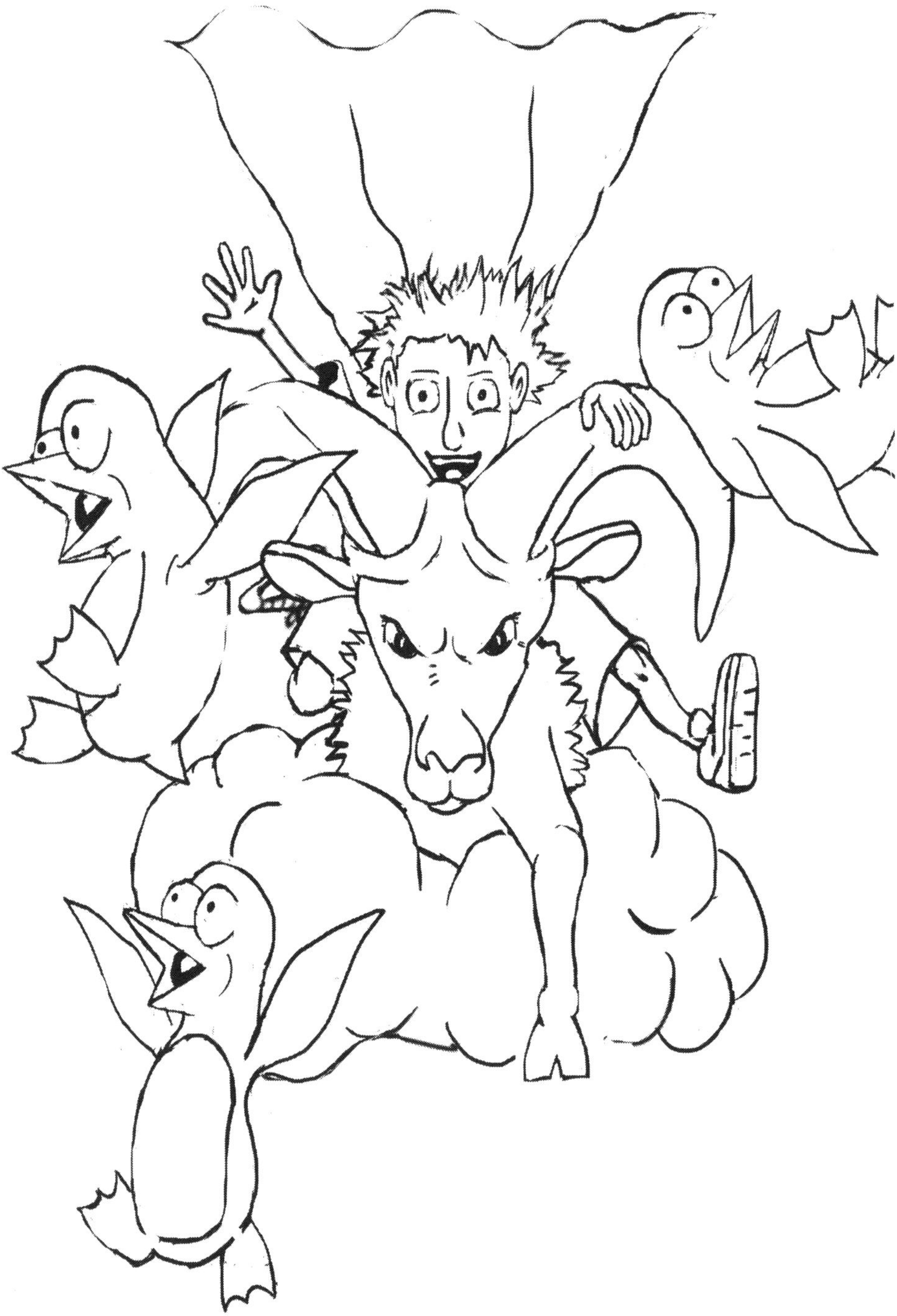

CHAPTER 9

Aftermath

Filbert floated in a jail cell that was just barely big enough to hold him. In the next cell, the penguins lay passed out, snoring obnoxiously. Everything Filbert was trying to accomplish had completely fallen apart. He'd missed the inspection, he still didn't know how he could ever face his parents again, and worst of all, here he was, rotting in prison.

A door down the hall opened. It was Cornelius escorted by a guard. When they got to Filbert's cell, the guard dragged over a chair, handed it to Cornelius, and said, "Here, you got 20 minutes." Then he walked back down the hall through the door and locked it with a loud *CLINK!*

"I'm sorry," was all that Filbert could think to say.

"Thank you for that, but sorry isn't going to fix everything this time," said Cornelius.

"Is Lulu okay?"

Squirrel Trouble

"She's fine. She's at home cleaning out the chicken coop as part of her punishment for disobeying me and helping make such a huge mess of things."

"What about your nephews?"

"They're home, safe, but The Tiniest Pig is very upset. He's refusing to change his underwear until you're released."

They got down to business, discussing Filbert's predicament. Cornelius wasn't very happy with Filbert for sneaking away and getting caught by the police. He was even more upset when he found out that Filbert had disobeyed his parents and run away. Plus, there was the matter of the inspection. The inspector said that missing the second appointment was the final straw and that since Cornelius had an unlicensed whale he was going to revoke his licenses for the chickens. Filbert began to cry.

"Filbert, I know things look bleak right now, but I'll stand by you and help you get out of here and back home," reassured Cornelius.

"Home," Filbert sighed. "I can't go back there."

"What do you mean? Your parents still love you, Filbert. Even if they are angry with you."

"What about your company? I've ruined everything," Filbert moaned.

"Stop that now. You didn't ruin everything. You made some big mistakes, but we'll do what we can to fix them. As for my company, I'm not sure what's going to happen. I'll figure something out." There was a sadness in Cornelius's voice that worried Filbert.

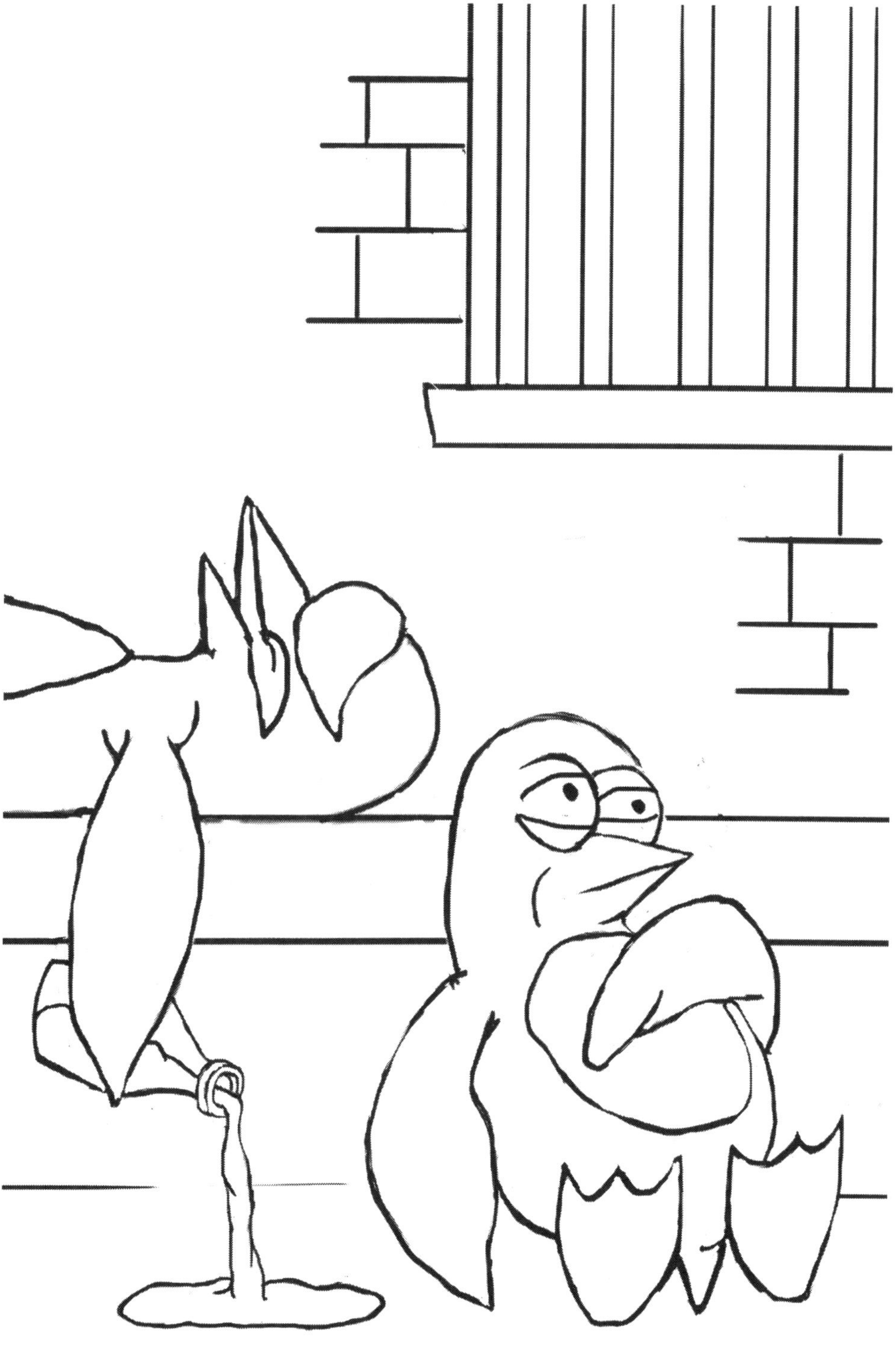

Squirrel Trouble

A couple of hours later Filbert was in front of a judge. They had to hold the proceedings outside because Filbert couldn't fit through the door of the courthouse. Cornelius was by his side. On the other side was Inspector McStinkle. He spoke for The City. Filbert was charged with creating a public disturbance and resisting arrest, as well as failing to show for a city-mandated inspection on two occasions. After the charges were announced, it was time for Filbert to enter a plea of guilty or not guilty. Just as Cornelius was about to speak for Filbert, a large crowd of people and squirrels showed up.

The crowd was chanting, "Free Filbert! Free Filbert!"

The judge banged his gavel and called for order. The police tried to keep them back, but they were greatly outnumbered. The crowd would not leave until they were heard. The judge finally gave in and agreed to listen to what they had to say.

Stepping up to speak for the crowd was a tall man with a purple Mohawk and the word "love" tattooed across his face. He declined to give his name because he didn't wish to be identified. On his shoulder was Commissioner Tiny Fingers. Together, they recounted the mayhem created by the drunken penguins which led to the fire in the park. Included in the retelling was how Filbert, Lulu, and a donkey were trying to organize people to help fight the fire when the penguins turned on them. Also included was how a mysterious caped boy riding a goat had come to their rescue. Finally, they described Filbert single-finnedly keeping the fire contained until the fire fighters arrived.

Aftermath

"Considering this new information, I think it would be in poor judgment to proceed with the charges against Filbert," announced the judge, causing cheers to erupt from the crowd. "What do you think, Inspector McStinkle?"

"I wholeheartedly agree, Your Honor," said McStinkle. There were more cheers. "I believe that not only should the charges against Filbert be dropped but that he should be granted free reign of The City and recognized as a hero! I would also like to formally announce that there will be no charges brought against Cornelius Featherthief and that the licenses for his chickens and business shall remain valid."

Once the crowd quieted down enough for Commissioner Tiny Fingers to be heard, he made an announcement of his own: "I declare the Destroyer an official Friend to the Squirrels of Dirty Dog Park!"

Filbert and Cornelius thanked Inspector McStinkle, the judge, and the crowd.

It was time to get Filbert back home. Cornelius jumped up onto Filbert's back and they set out for the ocean. The crowd followed, cheering and chanting along the way. Filbert suggested they stop off and tell Lulu the good news.

"Oh no," said Cornelius. "She's grounded for a month! That means no friend visits for her, including you. We need to get you back to your parents. I'll tell her the good news when I get home."

Once they reached the beach, Filbert thanked the crowd again. Cornelius and Commissioner Tiny Fingers rented a small boat, while Filbert went ahead to find his parents.

Squirrel Trouble

Cornelius and the Commissioner set sail for buoy 159; there they would await Filbert and his family.

Filbert was excited to go home a hero, but as he plunged beneath the surface of the water, he remembered that he'd left after his parents had specifically forbidden him to. With every flick of his powerful tail, Filbert's fear grew. By the time he reached the house, tears were streaming down his face. Filbert crashed through the front door.

"Mama!" wailed Filbert. "I'm home!"

Without a word, Edweena scooped up her missing son in her massive fins and held him tight. Filbert cried and apologized. He was truly sorry. Mama cried along with him, thankful that he was home safe. Dad and Roger joined in. Filbert's fear of losing his family's love melted away. The story of his adventure poured out of him and the family listened.

"This is not going to go unpunished, young man," said his father sternly, wiping tears of joy from his eyes.

"We're glad you're home, but you went too far this time. We told you not to go, but you did anyway," Mother agreed.

Roger looked a bit uncomfortable at the mention of punishment. He gave his brother a wink and quietly swam away, mumbling something about feeding the clams.

"I'm just so happy that you still love me," said Filbert. "Cornelius and the leader of the squirrels are up at buoy 159. Won't you come meet them?" Filbert's parents agreed to meet Cornelius and the squirrel.

The three of them popped up a few yards away from the boat. Introductions were made; Cornelius and Commissioner

Aftermath

Tiny Fingers told of Filbert's heroic deed.

"Your boy is a very respectful, brave, and honorable young whale," concluded Cornelius. The Commissioner nodded in agreement. "With that being said, I still don't think he should go unpunished for running away."

"Thank you, Cornelius, for the help and kindness you have shown our son. And I am glad that you and Filbert have worked your differences out, Commissioner," said Edweena.

"It seems that Filbert has done our family proud and gained some fine friends at the same time. We are grateful for all you two have done for our son. We look forward to having you as friends of our family," said Richard. "I hope you will excuse us now. The last couple of days have been very trying and stressful."

The whales said their goodbyes and left for home.

"Mom, Dad, I'm really sorry and hope that you can forgive me. I know I deserve whatever punishment you see fit to give me," said Filbert graciously.

"You sound so grown-up, my little guppy," said Mother. "I think you are learning to take responsibility for yourself and I'm proud of you."

"You know, in my day you would have gotten a good old fashioned whooping," said Richard with a smirk.

"Mom!" protested Filbert.

"Don't 'Mom' me, honey. I would have done the same thing, but in light of your heroic deeds, I think just a grounding and extra chores will suffice this time."

The next morning, on his first day of his punishment, Filbert

Squirrel Trouble

was awakened by Smeepy and Smarple. The clams dove into Filbert's bed, knocked him to the floor, and proceeded to hop all over his head until Roger pulled them away.

"Hey, what gives?" asked Filbert, still a little dazed.

"Smeepy and Smarple just wanted to say hi. They missed you," said Roger, grinning. "Oh yeah, that was for deserting us at the park, too."

Filbert just shook his head and smiled. It was great to be home!

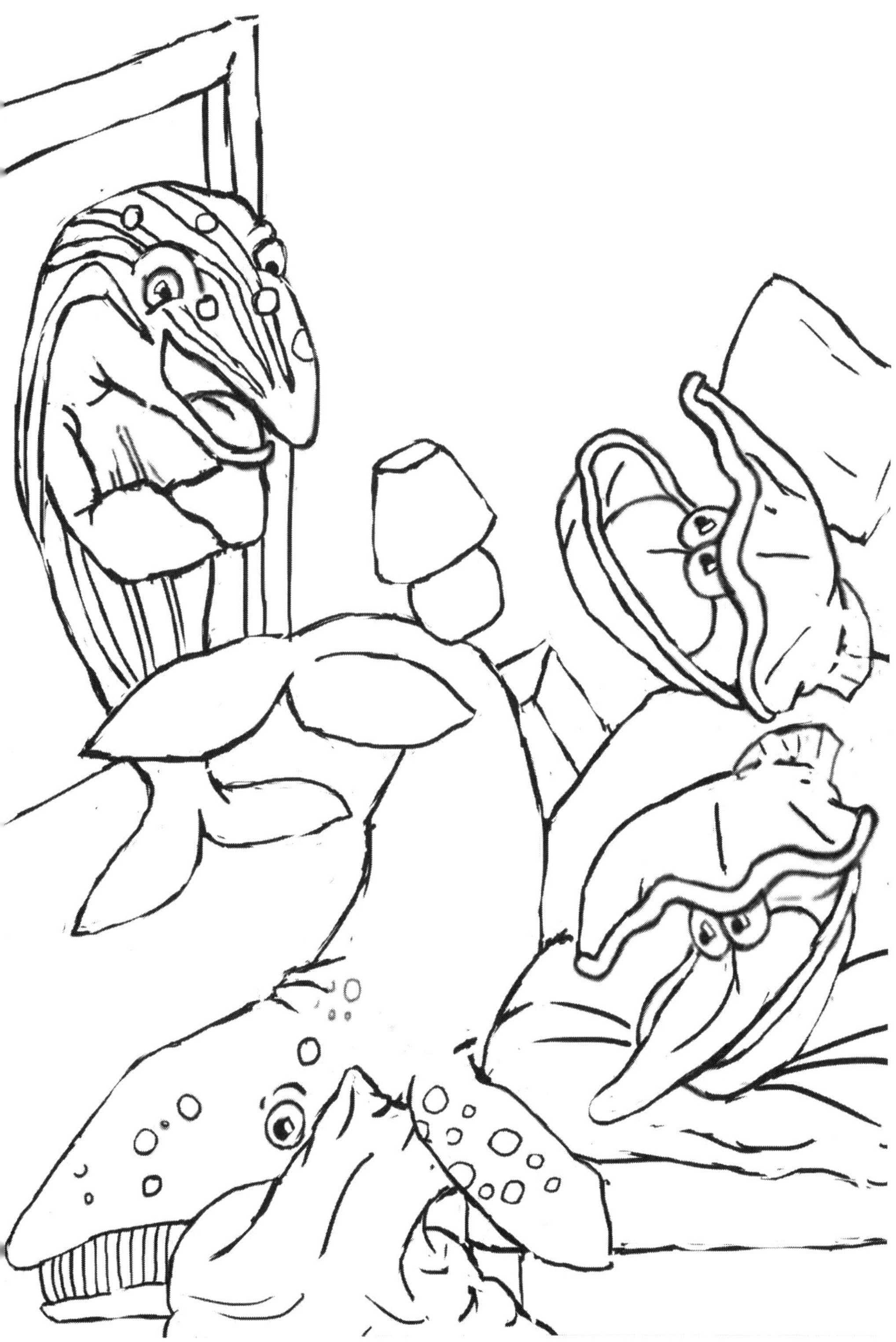

About the Author

Allen dwells in the enchanted, mist-shrouded forest known as Muir Woods. He is a mud-covered, miserly troll, who finds kinship with the toads and lizards that live among the massive redwood trees. His dank, moss-covered lair is dug from the burnt-out hollow of one of these coastal giants. With the singular aspiration of separating fools from their ill-gotten riches, Allen preys on unsavory, treasure-seeking mercenaries. He lines the floor of his burrow with their gold, silver, and magical items. The treasure serves as a kind of nest, where Allen curls up and snores boisterously, dreaming he is a mystical green dragon.

Booty Bombs

Squirrel Surprise

Slip of the Hammer

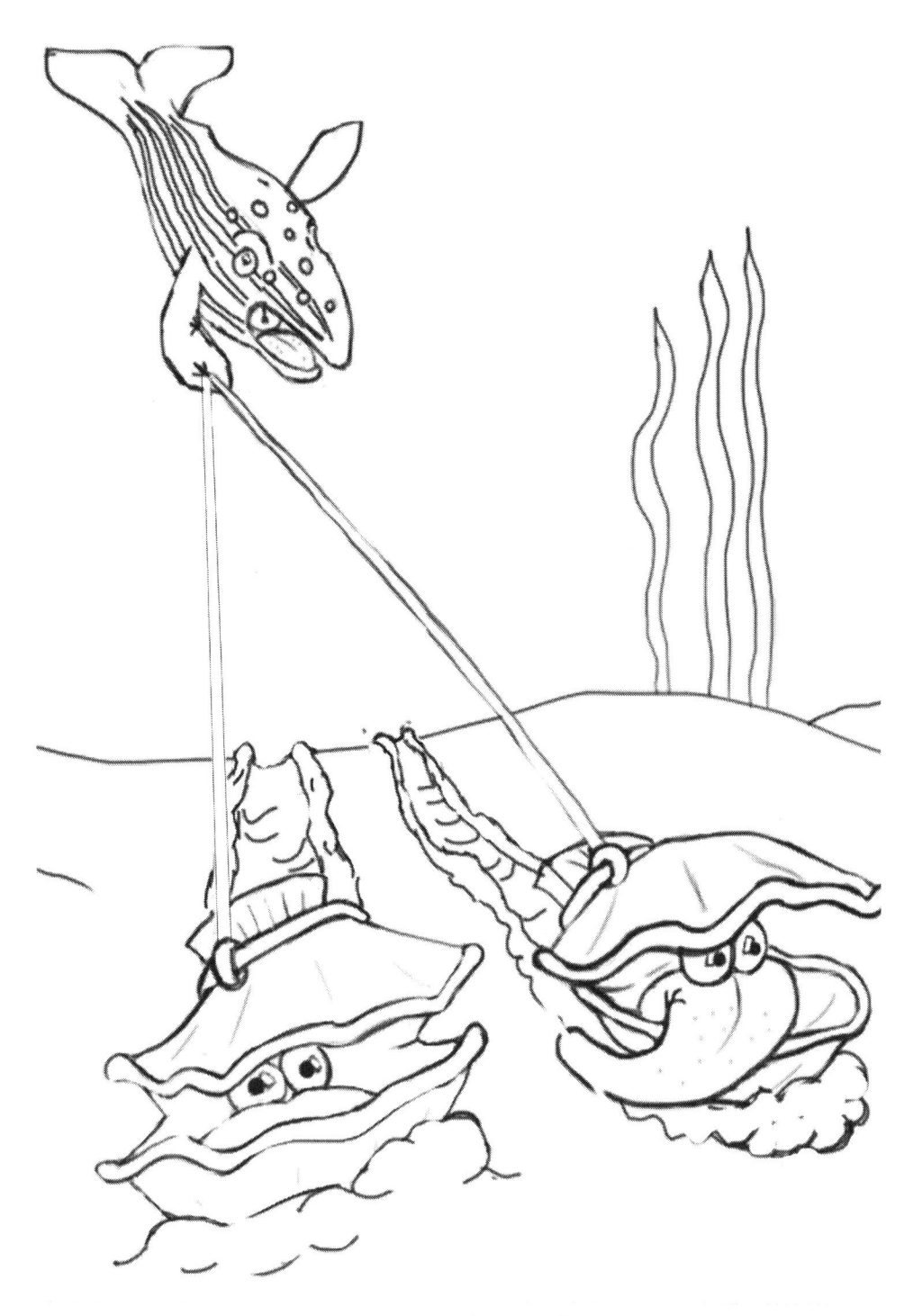

Smeepy and Smarple

Donkey and The Tiniest Pig

Slingshot Salamanders

Snarly and Filbert Under Fire

Squirrel Court

The Wagon

G.O.A.T.S.!

The Morning After

Roger's Revenge

Made in the USA
Columbia, SC
25 June 2025